How to write any essay and get a top mark!

(Or How to Hack the Religious Studies, Ethics or Philosophy A-level (& Politics and Other Essay) Exams…and get an A*!)

For AQA, OCR, and Edexcel, New and Old courses! Unit/Course/Specification codes: 7061, 7062, 2060, 7171, 7172, 2175, H172, H572, H173, H573, 8RS01, 9RS01, 8RS0, 9RS0 and many more!

By Andrew P M Yiallouros

Copyright © 2016 by Andrew P M Yiallouros (including cover image).

All rights reserved. The author's comments represent his opinion and only his opinion and no guarantees are made over the effectiveness of this book. No part of this publication may be reproduced, distributed, or transmitted in any form or by any means, including photocopying, recording, or other electronic or mechanical methods, without the prior written permission of the publisher, except in the case of brief quotations embodied in critical reviews and certain other non-commercial uses permitted by copyright law. All sample questions provided were developed by the author who listed all the possible questions that he could think of and then looking for where these were repeated by the exam boards. For permission requests, contact andrew@commonsensible.org. Self-published in Thailand through Amazon and other outlets. Available to buy on Amazom.com and all major outlets. Author's website: www.commonsensible.org.

Thanks to Sarah K Tyler who reviewed this work prior to publishing.

First Edition

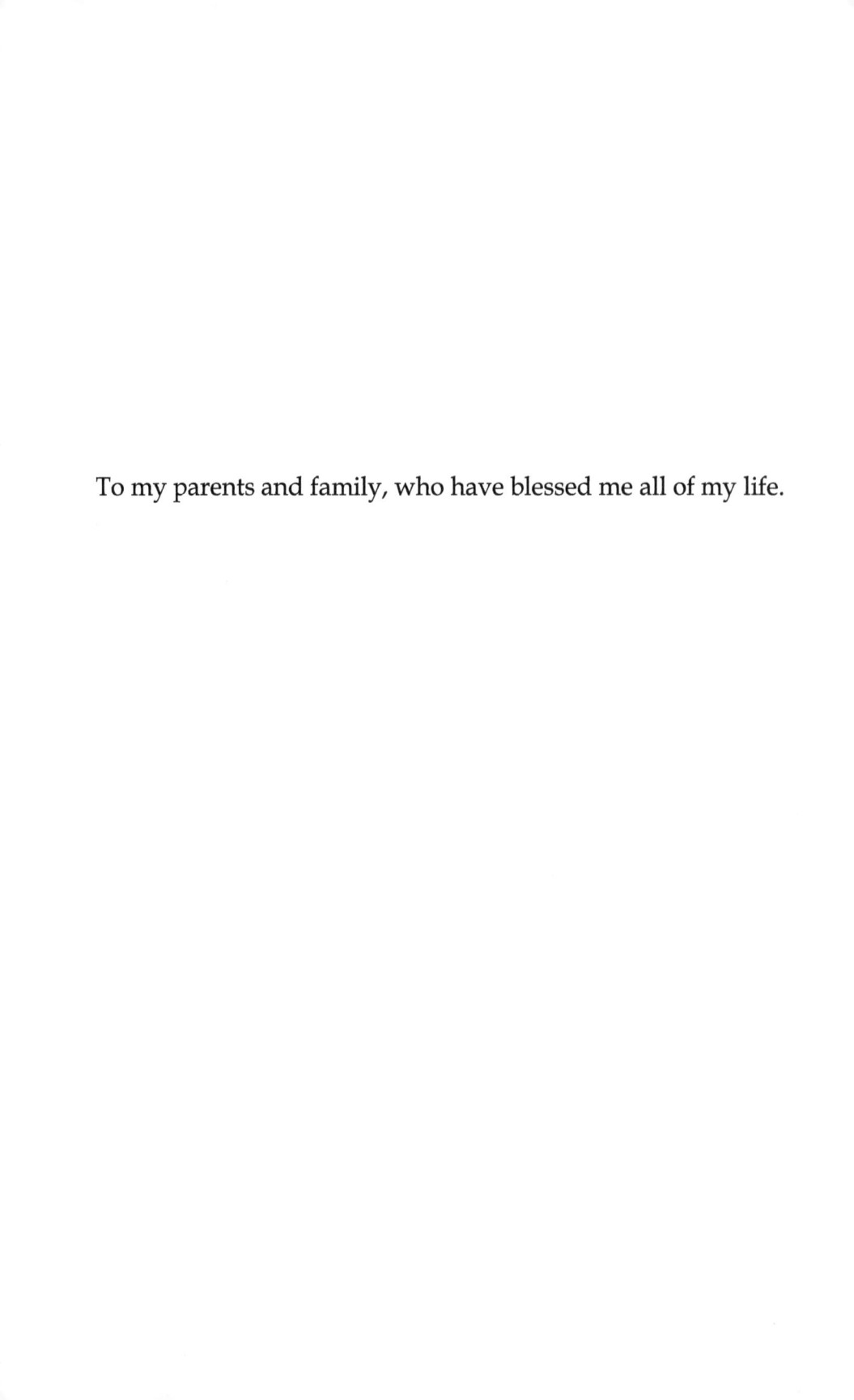

To my parents and family, who have blessed me all of my life.

"Education is the kindling of a flame, not the filling of a vessel."

Socrates

CONTENTS

THE BLURB

1. How to use this book
2. Introduction
3. You
4. Why Religious Studies, Philosophy and Ethics?
5. Confidence is Key
6. Forget targets and predicted grades, everyone can get an A*
7. Teachers and Examiners

THE SYSTEM

1. Knowledge Acquisition
2. The Basics
3. Writing
4. SPEEDL (AO1 & AO2)
5. Yes, No, Maybe (AO2)
6. For an essay that needs AO1 and AO2 (or AO3) combined
7. AQA
8. OCR
9. Edexcel
10. Revision
11. Practice
12. Exam skills/The actual exam
13. Questions and When AO1 looks like AO2
14. Lastminute.com
15. If it all goes wrong
16. It doesn't matter what the knowledge is
17. Recommended websites and reading
18. About the Author

THE BLURB

1. How to use this book

This has been written following the same principles that the system teaches. Paragraphs are exemplar lengths. The information goes from simple, to exterior stuff, towards deeper and more detailed, complicated stuff. I give points, examples and explain and so on. It has also been written with Neurolinguistic programming, self-hypnosis and neurology in mind. It is a journey that will last a couple of hours but stay with you forever. It will mean that you can hack any essay, forever. I really am giving out "secret" tricks and information that hacks the system so please use it responsibly.

So, yes, you could skip this blurb or other bits but you shouldn't - A*s do it all. To be an A* student, you've got to be excellent and that starts with you reading this book from start to finish (not necessarily in one go, you can go to the toilet, sleep and stuff) but, if possible, why not? It's only about 100 pages. There are some bits you could miss out, but on the whole, it's a complete system that needs to be read as a whole. If you can do that, read it all, follow what it says, and practice, you will do excellently at A-level! After that point, it's just a reference guide.

The first test starts here, to get over your desire to not read stuff, to stop being scared off text and so on…if you can pass that, you get a ticket to the top.

It's not your usual book, it's not your usual system, but it *will* work. They tried to stop me publishing it, that's how good it is!

For non-A-level students, and for A-level students of other subjects, you're smart enough to know when to read your own requirements when I use a word that doesn't apply to you. So you know when it's A+ instead of A* or whatever.

For teachers, this book is also vital reading and can help you hack the exam as much as your students.

Good luck, enjoy it, keep with it, and welcome to a secret guide or "hack" to exam success!

Any questions, please do email me at andrew@commonsensible.org

2. Introduction

Apart from lots of other things, I've been a celebrated teacher, a teacher trainer, a lesson & curriculum developer and a private tutor of Religious studies (or Religious education), philosophy & ethics (and politics and a few other subjects) for just under a decade.

I have also been an A-level (and GCSE) examiner for the same amount of time; I've marked for all the main boards and for many different papers and I have even been a subject expert and consultant with Ofqual (the exam watchdog) where I had to study and assess all the exam boards and many of the papers (I also advised on the changes to A-level and GCSE that culminated in all these new exams that have been released).

Finally, I've been a thinker, a philosopher, a scientist, a "knowledge hacker" & existentialist, *and* I've been a student (a lazy and disinterested one, sometimes a good one, but also a struggling dyslexic one) for well over two decades.

What does this mean?

I hate work, I hate school, I hate most teachers, I hate reading, writing, remembering things and most study. I find it all really hard. At the same time, I love it, or at least I am aware of how important it can be, and, I appreciate a good challenge. I also remember what it is like to be a student (and it baffles me why most educators seem to have forgotten it). I struggled, more than most, in my studies and I had to figure it all out for myself; being, as it was, before the time of "Special Educational Needs" help. I behaved well, I behaved badly and I've excelled and I've failed. I've got firsts, A*s and As, but also a load of lower grades, and I did have to retake some of my exams.

This gives me a perspective that most educators don't have; I really understand you and what you are doing. You the good student, you the lazy student, you the student who doesn't get it, or doesn't want to, and you the student with learning difficulties and more; all the different types of students there are, I have been or am you and…I really understand *you*.

To add to this, I also have that teaching, examining and educating background. The degree and the master's and the master's level teaching qualification; the 1000s of teaching hours (in class and one to one); the over 60 different schools I've worked in, studied or visited; the tens of 1000s of students I have met and worked with; the hundreds of 1000s of essay pages I have read and the countless hours marking and grading students work. Throughout all of this, I have studied that process so that now, I really understand what *they* want too.

Throughout all of the above, I've studied essays, how to write them and how they are marked, I've studied the examination process, mark schemes and specifications and all the little differences therein; I've studied how students think, how teachers teach, what examiners want and more…to cut a long story short: I have studied exams, especially A-levels, from ALL the angles possible and I can be your bridge to exam success.

Being lazy, being dyslexic and being a good student has all allowed me to figure it all out and find a shortcut.

I have used this study to develop a system, a "hack" so to speak, to help students not just pass exams but to get top grades. It doesn't matter if they've never got higher than a D or E, I have shown them my system and they, mostly, get "A"s or "A*"s. It doesn't matter if you are top of the class and just want to polish your approach, if you are dyslexic or have some other "learning difficulty" and need help (stupid term, don't listen to them, we are all just different!), if you have been lazy or disengaged for two years and now want to get a good result, it doesn't matter if you are completely confused or whatever, this system will work for you too. I've used this system on myself too; I took two A-level subjects I'd never done before and after studying them for 3 months at a semi-intensive pace, I used this system to get As in both (at a time when there were no A*s!).

It's simple, it's effective, it's short and easy to understand, it works, it does need you to do some study but, if you can absorb, mimic, understand and/or follow this system, with all the other things you need to do, it WILL improve your grades.

This is just some of my feedback....

"A great teacher with very good subject knowledge he is even more useful as a tutor because of his experience as an examiner with the board I am studying. He is also patient and reassuring with any topics that seem difficult at first sight ..."

"Rating: 5/5, Within a few months of tutoring with Andrew, I was able to improve my D grades to A grade work in philosophy and politics. Andrew has great knowledge in these subjects and is able to simplify hard topics. As an examiner, he was able to solve my difficulty in understanding the vague mark schemes and finding model answers. Andrew showed me exactly what an A* essay looks like and how I can achieve it by correcting my essays and turning them into model answers himself. This made me realise how achieving A/A* grades is much easier than I thought!

This was also my first experience of online tutoring, I was very sceptical at first but quickly realised how time saving and useful it can be. I am still able to handwrite essays and receive feedback from Andrew by email before even starting the hourly skype sessions. This way I feel supported throughout the whole week."

"Very good and very professional! An expert in his field and exactly what we were looking for!"

"Dear Andrew, Thank you for your help and I would love to work with you again in the future. Best regards M"

"Andrew was excellent, my son found it good. He tells you how to write an A* essay. He breaks it down so you can understand it better and he gives good analogies."

"I got an A in Philosophy and Ethics... I was really happy with the result and can't thank you enough for your help and guidance with the course."

"Hi, I got all A*s! Thank you so much for your tuition and I would recommend you to anyone..."

"Hi Andrew, Good to hear from you. "Y" scored an A*...So we would both like to thank you immensely for all your hard work. Moving forward, I would like you to tutor my other son, "U," who will be sitting the exam in June 2017. Kind Regards, R"

"Just a quick note to say that the year 10 essays you set came out amazingly well and, when I marked them, the levels were consistently high in both AO1 and AO2. The work you did with the students on structuring essays and adhering to the question has obviously paid off and they produced very polished answers to the questions - particularly the AO1 on Big Bang theory where some of the scientific detail can be quite overwhelming. Thank you for your work." E

"Hi Andrew, just writing to say that I got 8 out of 10 for the AO2…. I couldn't have done it without your help. Thank you." A

"Philosophy ended up being one of my strongest subjects this year after thinking about dropping it altogether in the beginning. So just want to thank you again for all the work you put in with me which gave me more confidence to do well." S

"I got my results yesterday and everything went better than expected, I got 100 UMS for both Philosophy and ethics!" T

"We cannot thank you enough!!!! N got an A*" S

"A got A in her AS phil/ethics…Thank you for all your fabulous help." M

"Thank you for helping my daughter, she found your teaching helpful, and got her grade for Edinburgh."

"Andrew really knows how to teach excellent essays skills. Also he is organised, reliable, flexible and pleasant to work with. He quickly figured out our daughter`s level and what she personally needed to work on to get top marks."

You can find out more about me at www.commonsensible.org

Or follow me on Facebook: http://www.facebook.com/MrAPMY

Twitter: http://twitter.com/PmYiallouros

Google+: https://plus.google.com/108952845114810816924

LinkedIn: https://uk.linkedin.com/in/yialli

Tutorhunt: https://www.tutorhunt.com/users/~waahwm/

First Tutors: https://www.firsttutors.com/uk/tutor/andrew.philosophy-critical-thinking.religious-studies.study-skills/

(I am available for private tuition, online only through Skype, so do get in touch if you want some extra help…)

But for now, this is what I am going to teach you here; I'm going to teach you what I've been showing my students over the years, what created all this amazing feedback, what I've learnt and what I know…how to get great grades, easily!

3. You!

Ok, let's get this out of the way first, as I've already mentioned, you *do* need to do some stuff! Quite a lot, actually…let's not beat about the bush. It's A-levels or some other advanced exam, after all, they are getting you ready for advanced standards, university and university standards (whether you are going or not) and they require a certain level of effort to do well. No tutor or teacher can learn it for you, do your work for you or magically get the information into your head, or *get* you good grades. You are the one doing the exam and you are the one who will do well or do badly. No-one can take that responsibility away from you and no one can interfere *much* with that process. No-one can turn a poor student into a good one, or fix your concentration, or improve your memory or help you read more, or take better notes.

I do get the odd student who thinks this, that just by hiring me or having me teach them that they will do well, that I can help them learn the stuff, that I can help them sort it out, that I can do the work for them. But I can't. I can only point you in the right direction, give you advice I've seen work, give you a system I've seen works, show you what I think or know you need to do and so on. Without *you* working hard, none of it will work. So, treat this as a disclaimer; *you* have to apply what I say to *your* life, you have to figure it all out, I can't guarantee you an A* or whatever, *you* have to read, study, remember and write and no one can really help *you.*

The truth is no-one can ever, really help you, ever….

Except you! You are the only one who can do all these things, and if you want to do well, you need to embrace that now. Life is a lot about delayed gratification, if you can understand that now, you will already be light years ahead of your peers. Yes, I could just eat that apple as it is and be happy, but if I waited, took my time with the apple and turned it into an apple pie or something, it will be a better thing. I could just have my fun now, mess around at school, not care, take the mick out of the learning or the teacher and leave school with poor grades and have that possibly limit my life prospects for ever (for more on this, please see the chapter about this called "If it all Goes Wrong").

Or, I could put off this fun, do well at school and then have lots more fun later, when I'm earning a six-figure salary. The runner has to suffer the stitches to make it to that finish line. These are just some silly examples, but if you think about this concept on your own, you will see that success, excellence and doing well, mostly, all require some element of delayed gratification, often through the vector of suffering. You work, you get paid. There's no pay without the work! Even in paradise, there's mosquitos and flies…

So, just for one year (though two is better), you've got to delay most of your normal gratification so that you can get a full "Hell Yeah!" on results day. Then you can absolutely smash it in celebration all summer long, go travelling or whatever fun thing you want to do. All you have to do is put off your fun for a year…pull out all the stops, go full throttle, study and practice whenever you can, limit your gaming, social lives or whatever…just for one year!

I remember when I was younger, a year seemed an eternity, there were also a million things I'd rather be doing than studying. But you have to trust me with my 38 years, it really isn't a long time and it is worth it. In fact, it's really worth it. Students or people who get top grades at A-level, pass higher exams or qualifications or go to university; are happier, healthier, richer and live longer lives (there's a lot of scientific data that backs this up). But even ignoring this, just think how happy you or your parents or guardians will be if you can do really well, even if it's in just one subject, or how happy your friends, teachers or school will be or how good for your future it will be if you can do really well! Options are so important in life, getting good grades increases your options.

Having said all this, I *am* going to help you with your understanding, your memory, your revision, your notes, your essays, your exam and all the things I say I can't help you with above. The point is, you need to do the bulk of the work and if you are not on top of it yourself, pulling out all the stops and trying really hard, all my help will be for nought. I can't guarantee anything but if you try your hardest and follow this book, you will improve your grades a lot at the very least!

On a related point no-one can turn back the clocks to give you enough time if your exam is, for example, tomorrow or next week. It will be too late at that point. That isn't to say that this won't help those lastminute.com students, there's a chapter towards the end just for those guys. But, overall, the earlier you get going with this, the closer you follow it, the more you keep up with it and the harder you study (read, research, note, remember), the more you delay your other gratifications, the more practice essays you do and so on, the better you will do.

To summarise: you need to understand and follow exactly what I say, but more important is to understand. You need to read (widely), make notes, study, revise and remember, you need to identify things you don't understand, work with your classmates or use online forums (see the website list) read further and figure it out (or get in touch with your existing teachers or with me), you need to increase your handwriting or typing speed, follow the specification and mark scheme, think about the questions and how you are assessed, make notes of facts, key terms, quotes, read original texts, use scholars and related people's views and so on. If you can do all this, exactly what I'm going to talk about in this book, prepare yourself for a challenge *and* work reasonably hard, then you have every reason to do well! Ok, pep talk over…let's get to it!

4. Why Religious Studies, Philosophy and ethics?

Personally, I think it should be a law that everyone studies these subjects. It's not about the religion but it is about the philosophy. Or rather the thinking skills. These subjects (and some other humanities) teach you how to think, how to analyse, how to interpret, how to qualify, how to critique, how to evaluate, how to deal with lots of information or data, how to distil and get to the heart of a matter, how to explain, how to understand, how to know and so, so much more; things you don't get in any other subject. They teach you how to write academic essays and dissertations, how to see and think clearly, how to see the fundamentals of a thing, how to be discerning and so on and so on. These skills set you up really well for most careers, from law, medicine, academia, sales, consulting and lots more. These subjects cross other subjects and teach cross-curricular skills. In a world of change, with a need for multi-specialisms and big varied data processing; this is a skill of growth for the future.

I'm sure you know this already but it needs to be said for those who hate these subjects (and were perhaps forced to take them). These people should know that these are respected, worthwhile and useful subjects that are good for you and for your lives and if you can just get over the idea of "what good is RE?" or "I hate religion or God" or "I hate philosophy or ethics" or whatever, accept that you are taking this course now and so you need to do well in it and that these subjects have a lot to offer if you just embrace them, this should help those students a lot. I know, we don't all want to be doing religion, philosophy or ethics, maybe we chose it and realised we made a mistake. But, we *are* doing it now, we *can* do well, they *can* help us in our lives; so let's just get on with it and smash that exam!

It's also important to say that this system works for politics and other humanities subjects, indeed, it will work for any essay subject that follows the AO1 (knowledge and understanding skills) and AO2 (evaluation or analytical skills) (or AO3 which can be synoptic or communicative skills) system (more on these later). I'll give you a hint, this means it will actually work for most, if not all, essay subjects. That's because most subjects follow this system. In fact, all subjects assess you by asking you to show your knowledge, understanding and evaluation/critical skills. Some do this with multiple choice, problems, practicals and so on (mainly non-essay subjects). Some want you to do it all in one essay. Some ask for you to do it in two essays, one focused on knowledge and understanding and one focused on the evaluation.

At university, for example, you're often asked to do it in one essay. At AS, it's split between two and at A2 it's variable between these two positions. Therefore, all you need to do to make this book work for your other subjects is find the specification and mark scheme documents for your course or learning institution and try to translate what they say into this system. It might look very different, but it will be largely the same; it will follow the "Show me what you know and understand" and "show me your intellectual skills" system. Have a look at the chapter "It Doesn't Matter What the Knowledge Is" for more on this.

5. Confidence is key

There's a famous study that happened once. In it, the scientists pinned at the front of the exam hall the letter "A" on a piece of paper. In another exam hall they pinned an "F". They then got equal groups of students, with similar targets, levels, predicted grades and standards to do exams in these different rooms. Same students, just different letters in their exam halls. They also did this with a lot of students, across different schools and different ability ranges. It was quite a big study. Guess what happened? The students with the "A" all did better than the students with the "F". What does this mean?

Confidence is key. If you think you will fail, you will do worse than if you think you will do well. I'm not talking about over confidence, false illusions or complacency, they have no place in any successful person's mind. But *belief* that you *can* do well, *really* helps.

It means when you are studying, the confident person will keep plugging away at it, the unconfident will turn away. It means, when looking at a difficult text, the confident person will think they can handle it and persevere, the unconfident person will give up. It means when you've hit a snag in your exam the confident person will overcome it, the unconfident will have a meltdown. A lot of what I am hired for with my private students is this, I bring them confidence. But they don't realise that they put confidence in me because of their perceptions about me. This comes from them, not me. Ok, I help that perception have a basis in truth, but it's still them doing all the work.

It's like that story of the lucky penny and the footballer. He always wins as long as he has his lucky penny. Then one day he loses the penny just before a match. His wife "finds" the penny and wraps it in a hanky and tells him to not open the hanky and just keep it in his pocket as usual. He does this and wins his match again only to find out after that the penny wasn't the penny, but a button. Your mind is your ruler.

Therefore, be confident! Even if you must fool yourself to do it. Be confident in me and what I say (that's part of the point of this whole section!), but more so in your own abilities, in your ability to action what I say, to own it, embrace it and to do well (that's the other part!). EVERYONE can do well, but you have to believe in yourself too! The best news is, you can easily believe in yourself if you follow the guidance in this book, so read, follow, believe and be confident; you can do, and will do, well!

Using mindfulness and meditation skills, which you can find out about online, can really help in your quest; it can help you to practice subtlety, deep thinking and mastery. I highly recommend it!

6. Forget targets and predicted grades, everyone can get an A*

I know, I know, this flies in the face of what almost the whole educational establishment think is true, what most teachers think is true and what most students think is true too; but…targets and predicted grades are a massive load of rubbish, sorry, but they are. DO NOT LISTEN TO THEM! (Teachers read the chapter "Teachers & Examiners" before you go ballistic…)

Predicted grades are given on a piece of paper a while before the exam. So, teachers have to figure out what you are going to do on the day, quite far ahead of the actual day in question. They may have to do this for a load of classes. They also have to do this in between all the million other things they have to do and under all the pressures they face (you won't believe me but these pressures had me up at 4am working straight with no breaks till 10pm most days). Teachers are overworked, overstressed, and yet they are under immense pressure to not let this overburdening be visible or look like they can't cope. They also have to keep their authority.

That's a recipe for disaster and it should be no wonder why many teachers just fake it, muddle through or take short cuts and then spend energy making it look like they are right all along; they have to do this "covering their backs" as they have to answer questions on results day (depending on their results). Let's be honest, they have no idea how you are going to do. (I'm going to get a lot of flack for this but I think the truth is more important; [by the way, I go into all of this "Educational philosophy/politics", let's call it, in lots more detail on my website: www.commonsensible.org]). For now, take confidence in this fact:

It's pretty made up. They will often just use the mock exam result. But as all students, but not all teachers (weirdly), know: who really tries for their mocks? I know for a fact that it's the same as when I was at school: only the really keen students try hard for the mocks (and there's nothing wrong with that by the way, it does help your final result to try hard for the mocks (see my chapter on practice), I'm not saying we shouldn't all be like those students, indeed we should…but…we don't all live in an ideal world do we…?). For the rest of us, we give it a go, but, well…it's not the real thing, why would I need to try really hard for a glorified "test"? I've got a million other things on my mind, not to mention the real thing looming, and I don't want to peak too early… And so on… Point is, it's not necessarily fair to use mocks as the basis for predicted grades.

Even if the predicted grade is given after a careful analysis of your past efforts, work and future attainment, it's still just a "prediction". It can't take into account a miracle (like you finding this book..!) or a change in effort, or a change in understanding. Ok, maybe all my homeworks, essays, class discussions (etc.) were rubbish. Maybe I do give all the signs of a "D" grade. But, until that exam happens, in my experienced view, anything is possible. I took logic at university once. The whole term I sat in lecture after lecture, seminar after seminar, completely confused. It might as well have been a course in quantum mechanics or Japanese; I had no idea what was going on.

And then, in the last seminar, about a week before the exam, something clicked, something changed in my brain and I suddenly "got it". I went on to get the highest mark in the class. For you, I'm hoping this book is going to be that "click". For us, we need to take away that predicted grades are just that, a "prediction," and, as history has shown us (except maybe Julius Caesar…which is a work of fiction…), predictions are a load of rubbish, it's really all about that final test, the exam, and until that is done, anything is possible!

Ok, ok, with that point now on board, why does it matter? Well, because these days most of us know our predicted grades. I believe very strongly that if someone is "predicted" (for example) a "C" grade, it's pretty stupid to tell that to the person. We are all psychological beings (remember confidence is key!) and it's no wonder predicted grades end up being right a lot of the time. It's like putting a ceiling over someone's head: "you can't do better than this". It also leads us into thinking that it is ok if I hit my predicted grade or worse. All it does is stifle excellence. I don't buy it and I don't believe in it. EVERYONE can get an A* and it is immoral to tell someone they will probably do worse than that. It's supposed to be a ladder to success, but it's just not used right in most places and it is much better that students always aim for the top and are pushed not helped to take the steps the get there.

It becomes a self-fulfilling prophecy if you do tell them a lower than top target. Again, I speak from experience here. I was a naughty kid at school. I know now that I was dyslexic (and served quite badly from my top UK private school). But, for most of my time, I didn't do homeworks, or did it in the car or bus on the way to school, or in the playground etc. I would joke around, sabotage lessons and teachers, disrupt and so on (don't worry karma got me back for this when I became a teacher!). I didn't read, didn't write and was just an all-round poor student. And I was told this, *all the time.* I was predicted "D"s and I got "D"s. I didn't think I could do any better, and my teachers told me this. I was in the self-fulfilling prophecy.

Then one day I decided they were wrong and that I would show them. I changed. I had to push myself, I had to do things I wasn't comfortable with; I had to read lots and catch-up, ask for extra help, practice writing, behave well and more. It was a process and it didn't happen overnight. But, it worked. I went to near the top of the class, became a teacher's "celebrity" for the most changed student, and I ended up with decent grades. So, don't listen to what your teachers think you are capable of, push yourself to be capable of more. You *can* do it! It's about being pushed, and the sad truth is, if you have a learning difficulty you have to push yourself harder. I think the way it works in school these days is that you are helped and targeted and limited and actually all we can be equal in is results. Some need to work harder not less but as evolution shows, that does create improvements. So if you have to do is push yourself and you can do better! But a shortcut is to use and reach the standard of SPEEDL rather than just PEE or similar, they are limiting!

There's a qualifier to all this. To get an A* or higher grades, you have to read, study, remember and write A LOT. So, when teachers see you not willing to read "because that's 'long' sir!", only producing a page for an essay when it needs to be 5 pages, not answering questions in class and so on, it's only natural for them to make assumptions. It's also only natural, in most cases, that these assumptions are right. If you have spent two years not willing to read more than a paragraph, not willing to write long essays etc., it is going to need to be a miracle for that to change. With the clock ticking down to that exam, the truth is, most students just don't have the time to change.

Our minds are just like muscles; they will do what you train them to do. If you train your mind to only read a little bit, to only think a little, to only write a little, that is all that you are going to be capable of. And, if it's the night before the marathon and you've done no training, believe me, you're not going to make it to that finish line! All of this tells us, then, that it's all about effort not ability. Those with the least effort, often, if not always, have the least ability and those with the most effort have the most ability; any other way round is false. This way round, everyone can join the party. We just need to focus on our efforts. Therefore, don't focus on your abilities, focus on your efforts! If we shoot for the moon and miss, we can still make it to the stars…! That's a key thing of this book, maybe you won't get that A*, but an A or a B is still good and within your reach. Maybe you will get that A*! Any other approach is limiting.

Thus, this book can be your miracle to change, but, you also need enough time. Ideally, you read this and instil it at the beginning of the two years. Second best is the beginning of the second year. Third and final best is in January before the exam or at most, half term of the spring term. After this point, it's not too late, but go straight to the chapter called "Lastminute.com" first. For most people, if you can read and action this book from January before the exam, you should have enough time to change but depending on where you start will depend how much extra effort you will have to put in... but...well, life is about challenges, playing the game and doing your best, it's the secret to a good life, to strive for the best. It all seems obvious really, but it needs to be said, so yeah maybe it will be a huge challenge for some, but it is worth it.

Finally, targets are even worse than predicted grades and everything I say above applies to them too. They have the additional problem that they are really political in nature. Schools get data on you when you join, containing your primary levels. They have to show progress (to the interested parties, Ofsted, parents etc.) throughout your schooling. They have to give you targets to give you something to aim for to help you improve these grades or levels and the two things (targets and levels) are intrinsically interrelated. But we all develop at different times. We all have stuff going on in our lives too. We also have to deal with school.

So let's look at this in practice; someone joined secondary school, year 7, on a level 4, ok primary school, not great. Theoretically, every year, you are supposed to go up a level. So year 8 you're a level 5; year 9, level 6; year 10 level 7 (but the GCSE equivalent) and year 11, a level 8/EP (supposedly an A* and ready for GCSE). Sounds so simple and right! But our student broke her leg, she missed loads of school, it's the end of the year and the teacher has to give a final level. The teacher doesn't have the last few test results to know her level so he guesses one. If he says she's now on a level 5 and her next level is below this, he will get in trouble or at least have to answer why. So he has to be cautious and choose a lower level.

As we know, targets are formed from the levels, so now her target is possibly below what her real level and target should be. This student now thinks they are below the rest of the class and it opens the door for the self-fulfilling prophecy. All this can follow you through school. What about the kid who is more in love with the fun at school than the learning. He thus doesn't achieve much and gets consistently low levels. But this kid isn't getting low levels because they can't get higher levels, it's just because they don't want to. But, he's still being told he has low levels and low targets.

What do you think is going to happen? What about a different way? A year 7 student is showing level 7s. If a teacher writes this on his final report, because the school has to show progress throughout, and because there's only a few more levels above this point, what's going to happen next year or the year after? So, he can't put a level 7 on the report and has to say it's lower. I'm not referring to any examples, I'm just showing a flaw in the system and making the point that it is better if a student forgets all that, aims as high as they can and then gets told how to get there and helped along the way.

All of this incorrect use of levels is wrong and immoral and is more about politics than it is about the students (again see my website for more on all this!). The truth is, most teachers don't understand or use levels and targets properly and they end up being a big problem. Thus, there's lots of opportunity for your targets and levels to be wrong and since it's a time line spanning 7 years, this can have a huge and negative impact on your schooling and attainment. There are good reasons for targets and levels, they have their use, when used correctly, but too much these days we get affected by them and this impacts our confidence, effort and our abilities.

Ok, another qualifier, if you suffer from profound learning difficulties, profound behavioural problems and so on; maybe an A* is out of your reach. I really hate to say it (and I have worked with Aspergic children or children who had so many behavioural problems no one would or could work with them but who, after a bit of help from me, did get the top grades), but it is more likely that if you have a very large thing in the way of your attainment, you are going to be limited. The good news? This only applies to a few per cent of the population. Roughly, 99% of you *can* get A*s.

To conclude therefore, don't listen to them (on the whole anyway, unless you come under the qualifier above). I want you to separate out all that school stuff and the exam. They don't *have* to be related. What is important is that you are in that 99%, you give yourself enough time, you follow this book and you believe in yourself.

I know this is true because I really do help "E" or "D" grade students get an "A*". You know how I do that? By ignoring all that came before, all the targets, predictions, all that school stuff and just starting again, exactly as I'm going to show you in this book! All we need is enough time and enough effort and a map to follow. You're in charge of the first two, this book is your map to follow!

New grade and exam changes

Another example of the primacy of politics and business in education, I'm afraid to say. Again, I'm on a campaign to end this interfering in education and you can read about all that on my website, but for now all you need to know is from 2017 GCSE A* to G will be grades 9 to 1, A-level will remain unchanged. There are new A-levels now with some still to start, and they follow the new system of no resits and a focus on the A2 rather than the AS being equal and related to it; AS will be stand alone. There's also some "mathematical" changes that affect "A*s" but the aim is that it is all comparable to previous years so basically don't worry too much about any of it. If you are interested, you can read more about all this here: https://ofqual.blog.gov.uk/2015/08/14/a-level-awarding-in-2016-and-2017/ and on the exam boards' websites. I'll also update this book as things develop.

7. Teachers and Examiners

This is an important part of this section. Teachers and examiners are human, they have lives, aims, desires, they have problems, like the rest of us, they make mistakes, they get tired, stressed and so on. It's important because if you can understand this, you can use it to your advantage. Examiners have to mark 100s of essays. Some have to mark 1000s. Some do more than one paper so they might mark tens of 1000s of pages. They have deadlines, sick cats, school work, birthdays, private lives and so on. So, if you can make it easier for the examiner then you should; it's going to benefit you in the final analysis.

If you can write legibly, it's going to help me credit the whole essay. If I can't read all of it, I can't credit all of it. Ok, we're pretty good at bad hand writing and there are systems in place to aid in this, but we are also under pressure to mark and level the work in front of us so if you can make it easier for us to do this by writing legibly, you should. Sometimes, just one illegible word can mean I don't get the point of the whole sentence and so I can't credit it. This can have a big effect over the whole essay. Also, we are psychological beings as much as you are and it is hard (even though we always try) to not judge a book, a little bit, by its cover. Bad hand writing sends a message that you don't care, that you are not a good student and it *can* have an effect. I'm not saying it does have an effect, I'm just saying it *can*.

So, if you're aiming for excellence, you need to remove as many of the variables as you can to maximise your success potential, and writing neatly is thus an easy win. This one needs a bit of time too. If your handwriting is bad in the January before the exam, you're going to really struggle to improve it in time. If it's really bad and there is no hope for you, I have to say, it will probably be ok, this is not a big thing, but it can also be wise to try to secure the right to type your exam (please see the chapter on "Writing" for more on this).

On a similar point, but also more importantly, you should make it easy for me to read your work. This isn't about the handwriting. Structure, paragraphs, grammar, punctuation are super important. Pay special attention to the chapters below that are coming up; they're some of the most important parts in the book and they will give you a system to deal with this. For now I want to get this point across: if I can see clearly that each paragraph is answering the question, that I am taken on a clear journey from introduction to conclusion, focused on the question, with clear examples of knowledge , understanding and/or evaluation/analysis, that there is a structure to your essay that can almost be skim read because it is so clear and well laid out, if it's simple to see that this is an A* candidate writing an A* essay and so on; you are going to maximise your potential. With it all being based on humans with a rough idea of what level and essay is, what perhaps an A* essay or top level answer should look like, and then fitting essays to that idea; it's always going to be a hack to make your essay look right and have to fit that idea! That doesn't mean you're trying to fake it, it does mean you are using everything I say in this book to naturally fit that idea!

Another question that has been around since I was at school is, how much should we assume the examiner knows? The answer is, you have to have some teaching or similar experience in the subject you are marking for. This means, it's more than likely a religious studies, philosophy or ethics teacher is marking your work. So, no, you don't have to explain *everything*! You do have to show me what you know and understand. This means, you do have to define some key terms, but not all of them. You do have to explain stuff, but not every little detail. I don't need to know that Kant took a walk at the same time every day; I know that and the exam is not about showing off knowledge or telling me a story like I'm a child who knows nothing about RS, philosophy or ethics.

If it answers the question, it should go in. If, linked to the question, it's an opportunity to gain credit for knowledge/understanding/evaluation etc. it should go in. If it's an important term, fact, detail, important to the question you are being asked, it should be defined, explained and/or elaborated on. I go into detail on this in the chapter on "writing". For now, take away that you are writing an essay to your equals and so you should assume we know what you know. What you do have to do is put down information/writing tied to the question. If I was allowed to tattoo, on your arm, one thing that will help you in your exam, it would be that: *just answer the bloody question!* Focus on the question!!!

Character wise, examiners are mostly really, really lovely people, way nicer than teachers! All of them have your interests at heart, they know how important these exams are, how your university, your teachers' performance reviews, your lives and more are on the line.

They know you are a 17 or 18 year old and you only have around an hour and a half to show the learning of two years; it's something I always hear in standardisation meetings: "Is this good enough for a 17 or 18 year old writing for an hour and a half?" (and the answer is often a yes!). They know that people panic, make mistakes and have meltdowns. They are trained at seeing the diamond underneath the coal. They are generous people. They want to give you marks, they want to give out all A*s if they could and they want the best for you. We also want to be fair. This all means, we follow positive marking.

We are looking to positively mark your work, there is no taking away of marks, just marks we cannot give. All you need to do is maximise the positive and minimise the negative: if half your essay is off topic, I can't really credit that bit. If it's all focused on the question and is relevant, I *have* to credit all of it. Also, if you said, "It's easier for a kangaroo to pass through the eye of a needle…than a rich man…"; we know you meant to say camel. We can ignore kangaroo and read camel. If you get mixed up and write the wrong word in the conclusion, a word which might ruin the conclusion, we can see you didn't mean to write that word and we can mark it positively; *obviously not if you do it all the time!* We follow very strict and well thought out guidance that gives you the best advantage. So relax a little…we're not out to get you; in fact we are out to help you as best we can. Examining is an art rather than a science, you can use that to your advantage by following this book!

As for teachers? Well, they have different desires, agendas and obsessions. A teacher, probably, loves their subject, or they may not be an expert in it so panics a little, or they may just want to do things "properly". This means that teachers often want students to know *everything*! They can be really focused on the knowledge, that is their job after all; to teach. They might also be more focused on the discussion or something else like behaviour (!) and so on. The problem with all this is, the most important part, the exam, can get glossed over or ignored. It also leaves students swamped by knowledge (or discussion) without any idea what to do with it (the bulk of the private students I see). It can also have students, quite frankly, knowing things that they don't need to know, or, at worst, not knowing what they need to know. If we look at Aquinas' natural law: there are, literally, 100s if not 1000s of books written on this topic. If I just took one of those books, it's going to be significantly more information than you could possibly write down in a 45 minute essay. But a teacher, thinking they are doing the right thing, may try to teach you all of that information. For them, it's all important.

For me, the only knowledge that is important is what the specification and mark scheme says is important and, more important than this, what the question is asking for. The specification is somewhat vague to underline this. We don't want to limit your study of "Primary and secondary precepts" but we also only really need you to know enough about it to understand it and to use it in a question. So, the specification doesn't say "You need to know *everything* about primary and secondary precepts", it just says "you need to know *about* Primary and secondary precepts" or something along those lines. Again, this is an opportunity for you, and I will get into this in the chapter on "Knowledge Acquisition". For now, know that teachers and examiners are doing very different things and that these two things can clash a little. It's not always like this, and a mark of good teaching is a good mix between the knowledge, intellectual skills and the exam, but, on the whole, in my experience, for teachers, the knowledge is first and the exam is second. For those who want to get an A*, the exam needs to come first.

The real problem is that teaching to the test is frowned upon (see the chapters on AQA, OCR or Edexcel for more on this!), teachers feel proud of their subjects and they want to emulate this with their students and get students to know a lot about the subject, to spread this love of their subject. This is really what education should be about; it should (at least to some extent) be about knowledge and loving the subject. The issue is, you have to do an exam on it and as these exams are important for your lives, for university and so on, in a decision between the two, the exam always, or should always win (always, only because they end up being more important than the knowledge). Please be sure to read the later chapters (and my website!) which go into this a little bit more.

The take away here is, until we separate out the life choice element of exams (the bit about them that can impact your life), teaching to the test will always win and *should do so*, sorry teachers. I want as much as you for it to just be about the study and love of RS, philosophy and/or ethics, but because of that very important exam at the end, it is better for the student if I focus on getting them an "A*" and put the knowledge second and fit it around that aim.

To my fellow teachers, I expect some of this is controversial and is only an opinion (and I invite discussion through www.commonsensible.org), but the point for the students is, that the education system *can* work against our wards; a fresh approach is needed. And it works too.

There's another thing that keeps coming up in my experience about teachers. Most have no experience of being an examiner and have no idea what we are looking for, how the exam is marked and so on. I often get a student's work that has been marked way too harshly or just plain wrong, for example. This makes no sense to me. It should be law that as part of teacher training you have to mark some real exams. The exam boards are often struggling with recruiting markers and it seems an easy fix to that problem, but, more importantly it's a fix to the greater problem of this: how can a teacher reliably teach a course without any real knowledge about how it is assessed?

How can they have confidence in their marking during the year? How can they do the best for their students without knowing about the exam? Yes, there is guidance produced for them and it's not like they have no idea at all. But time and again I see practice very different to reality. Time and again I get an "A*" student who is receiving "B"s for example. One reason it happens is to not allow for overconfidence or complacency, or other reasons of caution or politics. But, linked to the chapter above about targets and so on, it more often than not saps the student's confidence and limits attainment. Closer to the exam is also causes unnecessary panic in a student which can really hit their grades (remember confidence is key!).

The only answer is "exam accurate" grades. The problem is, aside from the egos and politics, teachers are by nature, work and training; pedantic, critical, nit picking people. Sorry but we are, it's our job, we must be precise, criticise and motivate to improve people. But this also means it can be all we do, which has its problems. It also means positive marking is repugnant to most teachers; we want it exactly right. You can surely at least imagine the horror a parent or head teacher would have of us putting a tick next to some inaccuracy in an essay. Thus, the system is set up, so to speak, to have teachers marking (and teaching) one way and examiners another. It sets up teachers to feel the need to do one thing, when examiners are looking for something else. It's a shame because it's an opportunity for teachers and their students and once you've examined a few times you can interpret any mark scheme and specification so it is a lasting piece of continuing professional development.

The split comes from teachers mainly being in charge of formative assessment; the giving of grades that tell you where you are and what you need to do to improve, hopefully pushing you higher: they are "forming" assessments, like a mould. The other type of assessment is summative assessment, it is the end, the "sum" of your study, "Summa" means the summary of a subject, this is the one examiners are mainly in charge of. Your exam is a summative assessment.

What's the answer for you the student? Listen, ignore and dovetail (apart from changes to the entire educational profession and operation which I strongly encourage! Obviously, you can read about that on my website too!). Listen to your teachers. All of them, the pedantic ones, the keen ones, the non-specialist ones, the old ones, the new ones, the supply ones, the "rubbish" ones. All of them. Why? They still know more than you. They still have things to offer. They are poorly paid, overworked and belittled *saints* who have given up a life to give to and care for other people. They have the right paperwork, access to the right information and the best source of help. They are *your* teachers. If you can find the good in someone, you can create a relationship and from there you can always find good rewards. And there is good in ALL teachers.

Then ignore them. This is a bit of Neuro Linguistic Programming or self-hypnosis but you've got to imagine yourself as two minds, and in one mind you are listening to them and following all instructions, and in the other you are starting again and ignoring it all, as I will, imminently, show you. This two mindedness is going to help you in your evaluation essays too. Cultivate it, but, please, do not go mad!

Then you dovetail, combining the two, using your school work as the skeleton to your study, and adding to it as I will lay out in the next chapter…

THE SYSTEM

1. Knowledge acquisition

This is the most important part of this book. Why? Because you just can't blag an A* (but do see Lastminute.com on blagging it). You need to know stuff and a lot of stuff at that! Everything else can be shown to you, given to you, or can be practiced and mastered, easily, by you. You know, as much as we moan, it's easy to write an essay. It's not that long, you'll be writing way more at university, in a lot of jobs, or if you ever wanted to write a book! How to write this upcoming, very short, essay, how to revise, how to remember, how to take notes, all of those bits of your course, of the things you have to do, can be told to you and performed by you really easily in not much time at all. All this essay stuff and pretty much everything else is given to you in this book.

But the knowledge? As we have said, only you can do that. Only you can read the stuff you need to read (by the way, you don't have to read everything, there are some videos and PowerPoints and things available, see the website advice at the end). But, the point is, it's *your* hand, *your* mind that links to the hand, and only you are in charge of what is in your mind.

So, what to put in it? Forget the textbook, forget your class notes, forget it all, just for a moment. The answer is the specification. It is this document that all textbooks are based on, that your teacher's lessons, notes and everything else is based on. You cannot be asked to know anything that wasn't put in the specification, it's regulated by Ofqual. For example, if a textbook had some information that wasn't in the specification, you wouldn't actually need to know that, despite our normal understanding that the textbook is the bible of the course (and it does happen, I've also been in a standardisation meeting where we had to allow pretty much any response as they had asked a question on knowledge that actually wasn't in the specification). Therefore, the specification is your bible.

Here are the links:

AQA: 7061 (AS new course) - http://www.aqa.org.uk/subjects/religious-studies/as-and-a-level/religious-studies-7061

AQA: 7062 (A2 new course) - http://www.aqa.org.uk/subjects/religious-studies/as-and-a-level/religious-studies-7062

AQA: 2060 (AS & A2 old course, last exam 2017) - http://www.aqa.org.uk/subjects/religious-studies/as-and-a-level/religious-studies-2060

AQA: 2175 (Philosophy, AS & A2 new course) - http://www.aqa.org.uk/subjects/philosophy/as-and-a-level/philosophy-2175

AQA: 7171 (Philosophy, AS new course, from 2017) - http://www.aqa.org.uk/subjects/philosophy/as-and-a-level/philosophy-7171

AQA: 7172 (Philosophy, A2 new course, from 2017) - http://www.aqa.org.uk/subjects/philosophy/as-and-a-level/philosophy-7172

OCR: H173, H573 (AS & A2 new course) - http://www.ocr.org.uk/qualifications/as-a-level-gce-religious-studies-h173-h573-from-2016/

OCR: H172, H572 (AS & A2 old course, last exam 2017, resits 2018) - http://www.ocr.org.uk/qualifications/as-a-level-gce-religious-studies-h172-h572/

Edexcel: 8RS0, 9RS0 (AS & A2 new course) - https://qualifications.pearson.com/en/qualifications/edexcel-a-levels/religious-studies-2016.html

Edexcel: 8RS01, 9RS01 (AS & A2 old course, last exam 2017, resits 2018) - https://qualifications.pearson.com/en/qualifications/edexcel-a-levels/religious-studies-2008.html

Now, maybe you're doing straight philosophy, philosophy and ethics, religious studies, New Testament, Buddhism, whatever...go now to the right link above and find your course. Go to the contents, find "subject content" of the actual course you are doing. This is what you need to know. "What do I need to know?" = This!

Next, some neurology. We have had writing for about 5000 years, maybe 8000, and if you include some symbols found in cave paintings, maybe up to 30 or 40,000 years. Our brains on the other hand have remained largely unchanged for about 200,000 years. So, for c.97.5% of our evolution, we didn't have writing. But we did have vision and imagination; pictures. Therefore, your mind is more "set-up" for pictures. It can process, understand and remember pictures better than writing or words.

Therefore, according to science, making notes, writing stuff down, relying on words, is not as effective as relying on pictures. What does this all mean? Mindmaps! That or some sort of pictorial representation of the information you need to remember, so, spider diagrams, infographics, whatever fits with you. That last bit is super important. It is your mind, it has its own preferences, and only you know what those are. Thus, if you are a pure picture person your mindmaps (or whatever you choose) maybe picture, infographic heavy (you *are* going to need some words in there, it's the nature of the course!). If you are more of a listy, wordy, notey person, then your mindmap (I'm going to stay with this term as I think mindmaps are the best) will be more word heavy. It's really important that you remember we are all different, so find what works for you, you will need to figure out your learning style. Either way, a bunch of mindmaps is way more effective than flash cards, reams of notes or a revision guide.

More neurology. When you read something, it goes in once. The mind needs space for living and new memories so it will "delete" memories that aren't used (or rather they will fade away). The mind also needs a reason to remember something, otherwise it will also fade away. Imagine just reading an Ikea furniture instruction booklet without any actual furniture in front of you. It's not going to make much sense, and you're not going to remember it. But if you read the same instructions with the actual piece of furniture in front of you and you use those instructions to put it together, you will find it much easier to put together the same piece of furniture without the instructions next time.

Get it? It's very important, our minds need a reason to remember stuff and this reason can come in the form of a use for that information. By using it, the mind embeds it and keeps the memory for next time. So just reading stuff doesn't really work, it's not as effective as other ways. Reading stuff over and over? It gets past the first problem but fails by the second in most cases.

Now, if I read something and then write it down, it's a bit like going in twice. Once through your eyes, and once through your muscular/skeletal system, in order to be written down. So, we get two for the price of one. Now if I also have to process that information, not just copying it out, if I have to put it in an order, in a structure and edit it; basically to put it on a mindmap in the right way, I get a third "going in" (eyes, writing AND the mental processing of it). All for the price of one reading. It's a good deal and you should take it!

On how to make your mindmaps (or similar thing), there's lots of resources on the internet, have a look if you like, but the best source with examples for you to see is here: http://www.tonybuzan.com/about/mind-mapping/ There is also software available here: http://amzn.to/2f7cnHe and books available here: http://amzn.to/2f7bQW2

Knowing all this, all you have to do is to take the information from the specification in the following way:

1. On one mindmap (they should preferably be A3 size) have all the things you need to know from the subject content of the specification, the whole course.
2. On your next mind map focus on one of those topics (for example Aquinas' Natural law) and write the detail that the specification supplies.
3. On your next mind map focus in one of the pieces of detail for the topic (for example primary precepts) and on other pages add all the other bits of detail.
4. Do this for all topics.
5. You now have your skeleton framework for knowledge acquisition.

There's more neurology to this, it's exactly how our minds work: they go from basic to detail. When you think about making a cup of tea, you probably just get an image of a cup of tea or something equally basic or similar. When you go to actually do it, your mind goes from this very basic thought to the more complex thought of how to do it. Think about it, you don't (normally) think of getting a cup, getting a tea bag, a spoon, some hot water, pouring, stirring etc., when you think of tea. You just think tea. The rest, the complicated stuff, comes later as you get closer to the tea. It's like this because of efficiency, you don't need to have at the top of your mind how to make a cup of tea, your mind just needs the concept of tea on the top and stores the detail underneath for when it is needed.

Your mindmaps need to do just that, start simple, with the overview, the initial basic concepts, going deeper and deeper. How deep is up to the mark scheme, specification and you but I'm going to recommend in a minute (but also throughout this book) how deep you *have to* go for an "A*". By doing it this way you are creating a key that will fit better in the lock that is your mind. It will work better than any other way!

Ok, so next you are going to add to this skeleton your school stuff, your class notes and whatever else you have. This is also the bit where you need to add the textbook info if you have it.

Then you are going to add your own personal research, newspaper stuff, "thick book" information, website information, key texts, quotes, key terms, scholars, different views, and so on.

With all the other stuff from this book, if you just did the specification bit, and remembered some stuff from class, you're looking at a "D", possibly a "C", maybe even a "B" for the blaggers.

With the school work, textbook stuff, a "C", more likely a "B" (and maybe an "A" for the blaggers).

With the personal research and extra stuff as well, as long as you follow the rest of the guidance here, you're going to get an "A*"! So, for me, this is the minimum that needs to be on your mindmaps. These mindmaps needs to be detailed but also don't go crazy, you need to be able to read it and remember it. Also, you just need to know enough to answer a question on it! Always focus on the exam!

There's one more thing these mindmaps need, the questions. This is linked to what I said above about needing a reason to remember something. You need to always have the questions and the possible questions in your mind when you are dealing with all this information, you need a reason to know it and the questions are your reason. In a way, the questions and the possible questions need to be given priority. Please make sure you read the chapter on "Questions," "Recommended Websites" and "Revision" below too, you need to read those bits, with this bit!

Ok, finally on knowledge acquisition you should see that by making these notes, these mindmaps, you are making a bespoke and tailored textbook for *you* and *your mind*! So, save your money, this is all you need. Just by making it you are studying the course, in a way, three times. Also, because you are engaging with the specification (one), your classwork/school notes (two) and then your own research (three) you aren't studying it 3 times but 9 times. 9 times of study for the price of one set of notes! There just isn't a better or more efficient way to learn something!

Also, it may seem like a lot to do, but it really isn't, you will see that when you start. Use indexes, contents and advanced search to speed things up, you never have to read a whole book! See if you can learn skim reading, it will also speed it all up. You have two years (or a year or 6 months!) to do it, so just make it a regular weekly thing, part of your study and schedule, and you will be fine. Once you've done the revision bit (see the chapter below) you will be able to "see" your mindmaps in that exam and you will be shocked at how much you know and remember and you will do better than if you didn't have them, all just because of these mindmaps! They should naturally tick the impending assessment of knowledge, understanding and higher intellectual skills like evaluation.

This also means that even if there is no textbook, your teacher is awful, your class too noisy, discussions all you do, and so on, it doesn't matter; you have the best textbook available, one that is written for you and by you. We have also now, nicely dovetailed what your teacher or school wants, what the exam board wants and what you want. So, really work on these mindmaps, they are the key to success and they are really worth it!

One last thing, when you are creating these mindmaps, try to observe, absorb and mimic the sophisticated, philosophical and scholarly writing; you need to copy this in your essays; remember, it's not GCSE anymore, no more descriptions or stories, it needs to be adult, grown-up and mature writing. On this note, let's look at this and other "Basics" of the system…let's look at what you are going to do with this knowledge acquisition!

2. The Basics

Academic exams, should be the easiest exams you face, not because they are easy, but because there is actually a set structured way that you can use to do well. Now, you still have to have the knowledge (as we have discussed above), and that requires effort and memory skills on the part of the examinee (as we have also discussed above). But, with a good amount of knowledge, and good command of that information, you just have to follow the steps in this book to writing a perfect examination answer.

It works for any textual response, really, but it is focused on the humanities and particularly Religious studies (or religious education), philosophy and ethics for the OCR, Edexcel and AQA. (It could also work for other British exam boards too, and it would work for politics and any question that's a statement and/or a question about how much you know about something, but see the chapter "It doesn't matter what the knowledge is" and chapters above for more.) We focus in on each board in their own chapters to show you exactly how all this applies later. But you can't understand that bit without getting all these next bits first. So, keep reading!

Alright, with these subjects, you're given a question and/or a statement, on the whole. The questions are trying to test your knowledge and understanding, as in "tell me about this" and the statements are trying to test your knowledge and understanding, to some extent, but mainly your evaluation and/or analytical, and/or critical thinking skills; as in "what do you think of this statement."

This means for AO1 (Assessment Objective 1), which is what examiners call the knowledge and understanding skills, you need to explain and show understanding. For AO2 (Assessment Objective 2), the name for the evaluation or intellectual skills, you need to show engagement, argument, and/or weighing up of things. All exam essays follow this structure, even if they use different words or mark schemes, so try to translate the below according to your own essay's requirements. (Some exams ask for an additional AO3, which is normally synoptic knowledge, the linking of other bodies of knowledge to the question or other intellectual skills.)

Actually, by law and by logic, they have to be the same or similar. By law, because it wouldn't be fair or right if one (e.g.) Religious studies exam was different to another. It also wouldn't be fair or right if one A-level was vastly different to another. By logic because, the exam is there to assess, summatively, a course of study. This logically, has to include knowledge, facts, information, the understanding of that information, the mastery of that information (the analytical bit) and the thinking about the information. It's really the only way anyone can assess whether you've learnt something. It's also a pyramid of differentiation.

The most basic thing you can learn is the repetition of knowledge. The next is the engagement with that knowledge, the extending it beyond just memorising something. The highest skill is the mastery of that knowledge, the thinking about it, adding to it, disagreeing or correcting it. Only top students can do all three naturally, but it can be *taught* to at least 99% of the population. Remember this hierarchy by the way, it will come in handy…

You can therefore understand it like this. For AO1, to get the "A*", **when you are asked to show knowledge and understanding**, it needs to be excellent, thorough and detailed, rephrased, reinterpreted, linked, owned and not just repeated. They are the first two rungs on our pyramid of skills/ability. This means:

1. You will have wide and above average knowledge = not just the textbook (in fact it doesn't matter if there is a textbook or not, as long as you have the specification, but see the chapter on "Knowledge Acquisition" for more details) – you will have really studied the subject deeply and widely (you need to use the internet to research the topics ("thick" books help too); I will recommend some good websites and books at the end).

2. You will have unusual knowledge = you must start to read a broad sheet newspaper or at least a newspaper, they are full of religious, philosophical and ethical information, it's current and if you can make it relevant to the question it looks really good. You also must start to note what scholars and commentators of repute say or think in your wider study (again see the other chapters on knowledge and websites for more on this).

3. This knowledge will be clear to you so you understand it, can remember it and apply it to any question you are given = your notes are excellent (mindmaps), and you do not worry about what you do or don't know; you know enough to answer the question in front of you and leave the reader with the feeling that what you have written is "an excellent or thorough attempt to address the question". If you follow all the steps in this book, this will be done naturally, you don't even need to worry about it!

4. You have about a minute a mark, a credit worthy sentence a

minute, maybe a large paragraph every 5 minutes, maybe a page and a half or more in 10 minutes, depending on your handwriting size. You need to say as much as possible that is focused on the question and that shows knowledge and understanding in this time. (See the chapter on Writing for more on this.)

5. Your exposition is excellent - that means using: SPEEDL and "Yes, no, maybe" (keep reading!). **It also means taking your reader on a journey, flowing from point to point, paragraphs flowing from and into each other.**

6. You must answer the question – don't go off track – the best answers will also question the question a little or at least be aware of the context of the question – why is it an important question? You are being asked these questions because they are controversial. You should also see that there is a limit to how many questions they can ask you and also that questions that are exactly the same can look completely different; the dark side of examiners (see the "Questions" chapter).

7. Give LOTS of detail, names, development; scholars and detail gets the examiner excited! But! It's NOT GCSE anymore. It only matters if Kant took a walk every day if it helps in your question; everything you put down must be focused on the question; do not list or show off your knowledge. Use lots of keywords, sophisticated words, have a good use of grammar, and English and punctuation. It is quantity and quality now guys! Spelling is *really* not important, spelling key words and course words correctly is.

8. To add to what you have written, think about alternatives (or even criticisms) to what you have just said – but for AO1 keep this to informative and not argumentative; this is a hard distinction to understand so we will look at it in its own chapter below.

9. Define your terms, especially in the introduction; also be clear with the reader and yourself about how you will answer the

question, what you understand from the question - if you got it wrong, it can be still be marked on *your* understanding of the question.

10. Help the examiner give you marks; make it easy for them to see you are an A* student! Follow all the guidance in this book but also keep intros and conclusions short and snappy and repeat the words of the question in the introduction and conclusion and at the beginning and/or end of most or many paragraphs. This also keep you on track and tied to the question, as well as making the essay more readable even if it makes it a bit boring.

11. AO2 needs all of this, but not quite the same, so make sure you read "Yes, no, maybe" too.

12. You need to give quotes, but paraphrasing is fine. Shortening words like NL instead of natural law is fine as long as the first time you do it you give the key, so the first time you write "natural law (NL)", *then* you use NL. If you are indenting, do it throughout, if not, don't do it at all. Try and have equal paragraphs but as you can see from the examples below (and every paragraph in this book), it's not critical. Structure is for ease of communication, so it's about helping the reader read your work. Same as grammar and punctuation. Finally, brackets, commas and semi-colons are your friend.

3. Writing

You need to write fast and a lot! I'm sorry to say that, in my experience, a lot of the times, those that write the most, as long as it is relevant, sophisticated and tied to the question, get the highest marks. Sorry but it's true. I'm sorry because until this point it is drummed into us that it is quality over quantity. But for young (and older) adults like you, it is both! Yes, it is possible to get an A* on a page and a half when everyone else is writing three. But we're not looking for possibilities, we are looking for certainty, and the only certain way to get an A* is to write a decent amount; to write lots of credit worthy stuff!

These exams are actually designed to be really tight on time. It's another way to differentiate and sort the wheat from the chaff. "A*" students don't spend ages thinking, or blowing their nose, or going to the toilet, or fiddling with their pen or whatever. "A*" students smash it! It is a race and the winners are those who are writing (almost) from the word "go"! So, to get that "A*" you need to be writing for nearly every second of that exam (focused on the question and so on…we will look at this further in the next few chapters).

Ok, so if it's a race, a marathon let's say, you can train for it. From now until the exam you need to have a pet project of increasing your handwriting speed. You have muscles in your hand just like you have muscles in your leg and, like the legs, they can be trained to perform better. For any homework, essay, note taking; you may have, you need to play a game (and have fun with it) of "how fast can I go?" Time yourself. Start to get used to timed writing. Maybe in the beginning you can do a page and a half in 20 minutes. But if you keep pushing it, training it, by the time of the exam you could double that or more. A good number to aim for is an A4 page of writing in 5 minutes, it's a challenge, but even if you don't hit it and just get close-ish, you will be writing fast enough!

This is one big way this system is a hack, if you write a lot, focussed on the question, with a good structure and communication, so your essay fits what the higher levels say in the mark scheme, they just have to put your work in those higher brackets!

Don't worry (too much) about handwriting. We can read messy handwriting as I've said above. It does need to legible. But it doesn't need to be neat (though the structure lay out, punctuation and so on does). I see a lot of essays that start neat and by the end the student is panicking, trying to finish on time and the writing gets more and more messy. But, you know what, it doesn't matter, those students might as well start messy and save the time. I can't stress that enough, time is your biggest enemy in these exams and you need to train yourself and write fast (really, go nuts!) in order to tame time.

Lastly, if you are typing the exam then you shouldn't be doing any writing, you should be typing and increasing that speed, just the same as if you were writing. I want to stress this, whatever format you are doing the exam in, writing or typing, this is what you should be doing throughout your time of study. There's no point typing essays or notes if you're not typing, it's the wrong sort of training; I mean, you wouldn't train for a running race by practicing your butterfly-stroke would you?! A lot of teachers seem to forget this and ask students to type all year and then wonder why the results from the hand-written exams are so shoddy!

Students who wish to see if they can qualify to type (it's not actually that easy by the way) then see your SENCO or similar person and include your parents or guardians.

Finally, there's a qualifier here, you need to judge the length by the marks and the space provided. For short answers, you wouldn't normally go over the space given. For long answers you should go over. So temper everything I say about writing with that and your mark scheme and specification!

Ok, with this all on board, let's now look at the juicy bit, what you are going to write!

4. SPEEDL

The answer is SPEEDL (pronounced speedel)! You've probably heard of PEE, PEEL or whatever acronym your school uses. Unfortunately, these are a good start, but it's not enough for an "A*". SPEEDL is. It is usable for AO1 and AO2 (but add in the guidance from the chapter on "Yes, No, Maybe" to your AO2 answers too.) It is mainly for AO1.

What is SPEEDL?

SPEEDL		
S	Signpost	Your intro and your first sentence for (nearly) every paragraph, repeating the words of the question
P	Point	The actual point that answers the question – to build your essay, therefore, all you need is a collection of points, they are the spine of your essay
E	Evidence/Example/quote/fact/detail	These two can be swapped around
E	Explain	
D	Develop	The more of these the better up to about 3 or 4
L	Link	Your conclusion and also the last sentence of (nearly) every paragraph, repeating the words of the question

Follow this structure above for most paragraphs -

For example: *"What is a pen"*

S – A pen is lots of different things
P – The thing I am writing with is a pen
E – I know it is a pen as a pen is a thin object that has ink coming out at one end when you push it on a hard and porous surface.
Ex – Pens use ink to leave a mark or writing on paper
D – some pens are blue, others are different colours and they can come in rollerball, ink and fountain styles.
L – Therefore, this is one explanation of what a pen is.

e.g. *"Explain the importance and meaning of the Greatest Happiness Principle to the theory of Utilitarianism"*

S – some believe the meaning and importance of the GHP is clear and very important.
P – without this principle it wouldn't be utilitarianism. It means maximising happiness.
E – Bentham, Mill and Singer all include it. They mean it differently though.
E – Mill and Singer alter it but it's still a foundation of the theory.
D – some might say just happiness is important but without GHP and its importance to Bentham, would there be Utilitarianism?
L – Therefore it's very important, though its meaning differs.

NB – this is a basic example to illustrate the point I am making... Your paragraphs are going to be much richer and more wordy!

AO1 is about explaining, telling me about something. My silly pen example actually teaches a deep truth about this. The most basic information you can give about something is a description of the thing, as you see it in front of you, for the first time with no other knowledge. But, remember our pyramid and mind stuff and our mindmap stuff, you can always go deeper! If I touched the pen, moved it around in my hand, changed the angle of my view, I could find something else to say about the pen. If I used the pen, wrote with it, tried it out, I could say something else. If I then looked at other pens, I can say something more. If I tried the other pens, I could say something more too. If I looked at things *like* a pen, I could say more again. And so on. The deeper you go the more knowledge becomes understanding and the more understanding becomes intellectual skills, so you tick all the boxes by expanding on what you can first say about something. You just have to practice thinking deeply to get it.

If I now say, *"tell me about Jesus"*: I can start with the basic stuff, A guy, lived in Palestine, dad was a carpenter. **This is the description, the story, or GCSE, "E" or "D" grade stuff, the signpost**. I can then go deeper; Talked about spiritual things, told stories, performed miracles. **This is the deeper story ("D" grade) stuff, the point**. Then deeper; One story, actually a parable, is about a widow, one miracle is about walking on water. **This is the detail, the evidence or** example, ("C" grade). Then deeper; The walking on water showed he was divine as only God has power over the natural world. **This is the adding more detail, expanding; explaining ("B" grade)**. Then deeper; However, he himself said he was not God (when the young rich man bows to him), although whether he was the Messiah seems less questionable. This is the even deeper information, linking, more outside of the thing you are talking about (Jesus) (you need to know about Messiah for example when the question only said "Tell me about Jesus"). **This is the develop, the A grade stuff**. Then; Whilst there are clear links between the prophecies of Isiah, other Old Testament prophets and Jesus, it is less clear that Jesus is divine. **This is more deep, linking, another develop. Still an A**. Then; One of the Old Testament prophecies talks of him bearing and healing our illnesses. **Even more information, develops further, now moving into A* territory**. Then; Therefore we can say *that Jesus was* (repeating the question in this final sentence) a religious figure who lived in Palestine, argued to be the Messiah, theologised to be divine, taught the people and performed miracles. **This is the link, the kicker, the punchline, the signing on the dotted line, the "have that your honour!" This makes it coherent, relevant, addressing the question, and an A***.

Now, I'm definitely not saying that this is an A*. What I'm saying is that with a decent sized essay, according to the time you are allowed, **according to the mark scheme and specification**, with every paragraph *like* that, much more eloquently and sophisticatedly done, more detail, more information, completely focused on the question, with a conclusion, and the rest of what I say in the book, that should be an "A*" essay.

Here are four model practice essays from some real student's. One is an exam A* (it is just like a real one that I know is an A*); it shows all the things I am saying above, sophisticatedly done. The other essay is from a student who got 100UMS in his/her final exam but at this point is not quite there yet. I am helping him/her get from an "A"/"B" to an "A*"; my additions to his/her really good essay are in capitals, hopefully it will show you the development of the system in practice. The third and fourth are "A*" model essays written using the system. *NB none of the essays in this book are perfect, doesn't matter, it just needs to be good enough!*:

"A*", inspired by an Edexcel, A2, old course question - 20 minutes

"The ontological argument must be a strong argument for God's existence. Examine this claim."

The Ontological Argument is an A Priori, deductive argument for the existence of God. Its first formulation was featured in Anselm's Prosologion with the following premises and conclusion:
Premise 1: God is the greatest possible being of which nothing greater than can be conceived
Premise 2: God exists in intellectu (in the mind)
Premise 3: Existence both in intellectu and de re is greater than existence in intellectu alone

Conclusion: God is that which nothing greater than can be conceived, as even "the fool" [Psalm 14] who denies the existence of God still has an in intellectu concept of Him as an analytic argument, the Ontological Argument "must " be true as anyone who accepts its premises has to accept the conclusion as the only logical deduction from this set of statements.

One of the main strengths of the Ontological Argument comes from its deductive, A Priori nature which means that accepting its premises leaves the conclusion as logically true. This is as opposed to A Posteriori arguments, which make inductive leaps in between their premises and conclusions that can be criticised for making conclusions which fail to logically follow from the premises. An example of the strength of the Ontological Argument arising from its deductive nature (making it "true by definition" comes from Descartes's definition of God as a perfect being. Descartes using his triangle analogy to prove God's existence – if God is a perfect being, and the essence and definition of a perfect being includes existence, God must exist. This is similar to how an essential quality of a triangle is, by its very definition, having angles which add up to 180 degrees. God must exist as his definition as a perfect being holds existence as an essential quality of this.

A further strength arises from the arguments nature as an A Priori argument in the strength of its logic. For instance, the assertion that even "the fool" in Psalms 14 who denies the existence of God most acknowledge his existence in intellectu. The acceptance and understanding of the statement "God exists in the mind" in its de dicto sense allows us to proceed and logically determine God's existence de re. Another strength of the Ontological Argument may be found in the strength of Anselm's premises. Most significant is Anselm's view of existence as a predicate, which is fundamental to the reducto ad absurdium which proves the argument to be true. When we assume the opposite of the conclusion to the Ontological Argument, we can demonstrate that it is absurd- if we determine that something "nothing greater than can be conceived" exists in intellectu alone, then something "greater than that" can still be conceived by purporting the existence of a being which has all of the same, maximally great qualities as this being but also holds the maximal quality of existence. Anselm exemplifies this via the painter analogy: we can all agree that the image of a painting in a painter's mind is inferior to the existence of a painting on canvas in real life. This further strengthens and proves the Ontological Argument as it shows the strength of its underlying logic.

Additionally, the Ontological Argument is strengthened via its proofs of God as a necessary being. This proof was developed by Plantinga in his "process of elimination". Plantinga first asserts that God can be one of three things: impossible, possible or necessary. Just as a square triangle is a nonsense concept, it is illogical to say that a supreme being's existence is impossible as that would be to say it lacks the supreme quality of existence. We can also rule out God being merely "possible" in existence as that would make him a contingent being whose existence is dependent upon another being –

this being would naturally be more maximally great as it would have existed before God, making him no longer the most Supreme Being. Ultimately, Plantinga concludes that God is a necessary being as this is the only view which is logically compatible with his definition, strengthening the argument by further proving that acceptance of the definition of God and denial of His existence are incompatible.

Malcolm further strengthens the Ontological Argument via his modal ontological argument which proves that God's existence must be true. If there is a possible world in which God exists, then He must exist in all possible worlds including ours, or his greatness would be limited rather than maximal. Therefore the ontological argument must be strong.

"A"/"B", inspired by an OCR, AS, old course question - 25 minutes

"Explain how a Natural Law follower might react to research on human embryos"

A follower of Natural Law might respond in different ways to human embryo research and it is not clear whether this theory can help us navigate such an issue. A follower of Natural Law (NL) believes that what is right and good is living with reason in accordance with the natural law of God. Using our God-given reason, we can work out what is right and what is wrong and also discover the primary precepts which reflect the divine will and their corresponding secondary precepts. In this essay, I will explain how a follower of NL would USE THESE PRINCIPLES TO approach the issue of human embryo research. GREAT INTRO.

Human embryo research is a very new field in science today and it opens up the possibility of new treatments for previously incurable diseases such as Parkinson's disease and even cancer; both of which claim millions of lives. However, it involves using embryos from humans which many Catholics, and therefore many followers of NL, would strongly object to on the basis of the Sanctity of Life, Playing God and Personhood. They argue that life begins at conception and, because an embryo forms around 4 weeks after conception, it may be seen as equivalent to ending a life as the embryo will then be discarded.

This poses a huge problem to a follower of NL because they would see it as a clear contradiction of the primary precept to preserve life. The primary precepts are absolute because they reflect the divine will of God so immediately, it would appear to a follower of NL as a clear violation of God's will. Furthermore, it may also be seen as violating the primary precept of educating the young because the embryos would be seen as potential children to educate; without the children to bring into the world, we are unable to educate them and enable them to reach their final cause of perfection. Again, it would be seen as a violation of God's divine will.

Human embryo research has the potential to cure terrible and life-threatening diseases so this would prove to be a dilemma to a follower of NL who holds strongly to the primary precept of preserving life – if millions of lives could be saved, surely that agrees with God's divine will? However, it may be seen as unnatural to stop a disease in its course as it is simply doing what it was made to do under God's command. A follower of NL would argue that we are not following God's will at all because we are playing God himself. If a disease exists, then it exists for a reason outside of our understanding as it is within God's Eternal Law.

In addition, using new potential life would be in conflict with the Sanctity of Life which states that life is sacred and a gift from God which we cannot and do not have the right to alter. God has given the gift of life, which is in the form of the embryo, so harming it in any way is an inherently wrong action. This point agrees with NL as a follower may argue that we are essentially blocking someone from reaching their God-given purpose. EXPAND ON THIS AND CAN YOU THINK OF AN AO1 CONTRADICTION TO THIS?

A follower of NL may also turn to the concepts of real and apparent goods by arguing that when scientists research on human embryos, they are essentially following an apparent good; they may think that they are doing it for a right reason when in actual fact, it is a clear contradiction of reason and natural law. EXPAND ON THIS. In relation to the Doctrine of Double Effect, a follower may, on the other hand, argue that if we carry out research on human embryos with the good intention of preserving life and eradicating diseases, it may still be morally good even with the morally bad side effect of discarding and wasting embryos. EXPAND A BIT ON THIS, THERE'S ANOTHER WAY TO UNDERSTAND DOUBLE EFFECT.

Therefore, to conclude, a follower of Natural Law would use their reason in accordance with the primary precepts and would most likely be against research on human embryos on the grounds that it violates the primary precepts, and therefore the divine will of God which is unquestionable and absolute. GOOD CONCLUSION, DID YOU LEAVE ANYTHING OUT?

"A*", inspired by an AQA, AS, new course question – Model essay of the system inspired by AQA's specimen answer in their mark scheme here: http://filestore.aqa.org.uk/resources/rs/AQA-70611-SMS.PDF – 20 minutes

"Explain why Natural Moral Law followers may reach different conclusions about the issue of abortion."

Natural law (NL) is the theory developed by Aquinas, involving primary and secondary precepts and concepts such as double effect and real and apparent goods. Abortion is the termination of a foetus in the womb. On first inspection it would appear that a follower of NL would reach the same conclusion on the matter of abortion as another follower; however, on closer inspection, there are reasons why they may reach different conclusions.

Aquinas would probably have considered abortion as wrong because it goes against the primary precepts of NL: to preserve innocent life or to reproduce. We could also argue that "to love God" would mean following His commandments about not murdering and so we would be forbidden to abort on this basis too. The primary precepts don't allow deviations. However, if the abortion was needed to save the mother's life (e.g. in an ectopic pregnancy) one could argue that these precepts would be violated but the other way round as the mother's life is also innocent and if she died she couldn't reproduce. Furthermore, if the mother's life would be destroyed by the pregnancy (for example if she was too young or it would destroy her career of being a cancer curing researcher) we could also use these precepts to suggest forbidding the abortion is wrong. Finally, we may not consider abortion murder and so this wouldn't violate a Decalogue and so may be ok. For these reasons we can see that on close inspection followers of NL may find it difficult to reach the same conclusions on the topic of abortion. On the other hand, focusing on the deontological nature of the theory, we may also conclude that we should just follow the rule and not concern ourselves with the situation. In this instance we may also come to a different conclusion than the above discussion.

The fundamentals of Natural Moral Law is based on 'good is to be done and evil avoided.' This also seems to rule out abortion. However, the primacy of this may necessitate abortion, eg to stop a 9 year old who was raped having a baby. Surely it would be more evil to prevent an abortion in this case as the famous Brazilian case shows. There is conflict in modern Catholicism as to whether things like abortion are evil in themselves or whether it could occasionally be morally correct to perform an act which is warranted by a proportionate reason. Proportionalists debate that an act may be objectively wrong but morally acceptable, or objectively right but morally unacceptable, so abortion could be warranted using a proportionate basis. Others may say that abortion is forbidden through the principle of Double Effect, because it can't be accepted to do a morally incorrect action to reach a good end. On the other hand, if we were focused on the morally wrong act of preventing an abortion which would lead to the death of both the mother and the foetus (ectopic pregnancy) we could use this principle to justify the abortion. Thus followers of NL may well reach different conclusions on this issue.

A discussion of the centrality of reason is relevant also. We may find that different people will reason differently and so may reach different conclusions this way too. Furthermore, looking at purpose, we could argue whether it is a 9 year old's purpose to have a baby. Most people, today, would say not. However, again, we find confusion as some would reason, whilst unfortunate, the 9 year old is female and able to reproduce and so has to have the baby, whether she survives or not. If she survives, it is God's way, if not, the same. This conflicts with different people's perceptions of innocence, God and reproduction. In this way then different people may reach different conclusions. On the other hand if we all agree with Aquinas' view of the purpose of humans and his argument that if we are not reasoning the same, someone is reasoning incorrectly, then we may well have to forbid abortion. However it shows, again, how on close inspection NL is not as clear as it seems and can lead to different followers reaching different conclusions. This is also shown when investigating the secondary precepts. Again, different people may extrapolate different conclusions about what the secondary precepts are from the primary precepts, as we have seen above.

Finally, a look at final and efficient causes and real and apparent goods raises problems too. What is the efficient and final cause of sex? For the former it is enjoyment and for the latter it is procreation for Aquinas. However, in a lot of abortion cases the efficient cause was not enjoyment (e.g. rape) at least for one of the parties involved. In this case the final cause could also not be procreation as the rapist likely did not have this intent. Indeed in this case the final cause is simply enjoyment for the rapist (unfortunately). This complicates

Aquinas's simplistic view of sex. For him the end result of the 9 year old having a baby would be good, as it leads to procreation, but many of us, today, would disagree with this. We may well then, reach different conclusions as him, if we have a fuller account of sex in all cases, including rape. Indeed, this complicated principle, doesn't really help us on the issue of abortion since it is so complicated. Using real and apparent goods, we also reach confusion. What is the real good of a 9 year old having a baby or an ectopic pregnancy leading to death? But Aquinas would have us focus on these real goods and ignore the apparent. However, in this case, the apparent good of the abortion seems more clear than the real. This also shows confusion and is why different followers may reach different conclusions.

To conclude, different followers of natural law may reach different conclusions on the topic of abortion because on this issue we are shown the difficulty of applying the primary and secondary precepts, the principle of double effect, the ideas about causes and real and apparent goods and how all of these, partly because of different reasoning, as well as different understandings, can lead followers to different conclusions.

"A*" model essay, inspired by an Edexcel, A2, old course question – 25 minutes

"Examine three important ideas in the design argument for God's existence."

The first key idea from the design argument is that as a posteriori argument (being based on experience) through the use of empirical evidence (evidence drawn from observation), we can clearly see design in the universe. William Paley famously uses his watch analogy to explain that if you were to find a watch in the middle of a heath you would clearly assume that it had been designed and how like the watch, the world was like a machine made out of intricate parts, all of which worked towards an end for the benefit of the whole and all the small adaptations in nature were, for Paley, proof of a providential designing intelligence. He then further assured his point in responding to past critics such as Hume in saying that even if we saw a watch partially broken (the same as we see evil and suffering), or a watch we have never seen before (same as the universe), we would still assume that it had been designed. Paley said that if something as simple as a watch has a designer, with him going onto show how intricate humans and animals were with his famous example of the eye and the arm that appear to have design, he concluded in his book "Natural Theology" that the universe would need a designer too, and this designer was God.

The second idea of the design argument is the fact that we can see clear order and purpose in the world. In "Natural Theology" Paley points out the fact that we can see a clear order in the universe in relation to planets and gravity and how this order is evidence for why god exists. This is then added to by Barrow and Tippler's book "The Anthropic Cosmological Principle" where they explain a point made by physicist Paul Davies that if strengths of nuclear and electromagnetic forces were even slightly different, we would not survive. This further emphasizes order in the world and with such clear structure that the world must almost be perfect for humans to live on. This also ties in with Tennant's stand on the anthropic principle in where it seems the universe has been designed so that human life would inevitably develop.

Paley also talks about purpose in the world, such as an eyes purpose is for its sight, which points to existence of God. As every tiny thing seen on this earth, even in its most intricate way such as am eye, is seen to have order in being able to have a function. Paley believed only an omnipotent designer could've created this. This was also Aquinas' argument in "Summa Theologica" where he argues that the universe must have a God in the same way an arrow needs an archer in order to reach its goal, the universe needs a designer for the universe to carry on living. William Lane Craig adds to order in the world as Tennant had previously done so in his anthropic principle. Craig moves towards the fine-tuning of the cosmos' life showing how constants or quantities of the universe (such as the balance between matter and anti matter) were to be altered by "less than a hairs breadth, the life permitting balance would be destroyed, and no living organisms of any kind could exist."

The third idea is that of Tennant's aesthetic design argument. For Tennant, the existence of God was based on the beauty that was in this world. Beauty, he argued, it is not necessary for survival and does not fit in with Darwin's theory of biology. The natural world is full of beauty, on a scale that humans could never copy. For Tennant, beauty of the natural world proved Gods existence as there was no scientific function and seems to only stand for human and Gods visual enjoyment. For example, he believed art, music and literature all contributed to the way we saw beauty in the world and yet we would be able to live without them. As Cicero says, "what could be more clear or obvious when we look up to the sky and contemplate the heavens, that there is some divinity or intelligence." Therefore, these are three key ideas of the design argument.

You should be able to see SPEEDL doesn't have to be done in robotic fashion, every paragraph. But you can use it like a ladder to build your paragraphs, you can skip a rung sometimes, but stick to the system and you will have an essay full of good paragraphs. Then it's like connecting the dots, easy-peasy!

Points

Thus, to make an essay, all I need to do is think of the points. It's the right way to plan, it's lightening fast and it will mean you will always have enough to say.

For example, *"What is a computer?"*:

* Made of
* Contains
* Hardware
* Software
* Power
* Can do on
* Case study

My points also go deeper, start outside and work in. It would produce a thorough essay on computers. How good it would be, would depend on the quality of my information.

What about, *"Examine ideas about analogy from the design argument for God's existence."* (Inspired by an Edexcel A2, new course question, 8 marks):

* What is Analogy (S,P,E,E,D,L)
* What is design argument (S,P,E,E,D,L)
* What are the ideas (S,P,E,E,D,L)

How about, *"'Natural Law's strengths are bigger than its weaknesses.' Discuss"* (Inspired by an OCR AS, new course question, 30 marks):

- What is natural law –
- Intro, Aquinas, context
- Main features -
- Reason, synderesis,
- Primary and secondary
- What are the strengths
- What are the weaknesses
- Related concepts -
- Internal, external, real, apparent
- Double effect
- What are the weaknesses
- What are the strengths
- Do strengths outweigh weaknesses ?

You should see that a high marked question needs more bullet points. It makes sense as you need to say more. Can you also see how I start simple and go deeper? And now that I have my points, I can use SPEEDL to build a great paragraph and a great essay. As long as I've got good knowledge and I've followed all the parts of this book.

Conclusions and Intros

These need to be short and snappy. A short mark answer doesn't need one. Introductions need to show you are answering the questions, what you understand by the question (define) and maybe identify why it's an important question. I don't mean saying "This is an important question because…"; I mean saying, "Some think that Natural law is a strong system that is valid for our modern day; others disagree." This hints at controversy and shows a high level of awareness. Conclusions just need to say, "and this is why what I just said above, answers the question, which was…blah blah blah…thank you very much and good bye". (Please don't write thank you or good bye it's a bad teacher joke, sorry.)

One last thing is strategy for your SPEEDL

* S, should be where this paragraph fits in the question, if it's the first paragraph, otherwise known as the Intro, the whole paragraph is a signpost. If its later, either repeat the question linked to your first point or link to the last paragraph if you are following on
* P, should be a point that answers the question, some can be only related, depending on the question (see above)
* E, should be an example or explanation of the point, rephrasing can also work here as can the next one…
* E, should be a fact, a quote, a key term, a piece of detail… you can swap this with the one above…
* D, should be an addition, something else, rephrasing, more detail, another fact, a related detail, or giving an analogy is a good approach
* L, should contain some of the question in it or link to the next paragraph or at least tidy off the paragraph

You could even modify what went into each bit, depending on your course. This is where we can really link to all humanities. For example, in History, E would be a source or an event. In English it would be a quote from your text or other related information. Can you work out what other subjects you could use this for and decide what would go into your SPEEDL?

New courses! Some have a focus on using source texts in the paper itself, so these become a bit like comprehension of these texts, based on philosophical or religious information you've acquired elsewhere. See how knowledge acquisition is so important? Also see how this makes it a bit like an English exam? Text given, talk about the text given. Finally these require some AO2 type sentences as they are often mixed; comprehension is about evaluating too. So with these types of questions (*check your mark scheme and specification to see if yours is affected*) all you need to is merge some of your English strategies for comprehension with the rest of what I say in this book!

My conclusion:

* AO1 is about explaining, examining, assessing, applying, showing knowledge and understanding.

* With a tight intro and conclusion, the essay focused on the question, with good information from your knowledge acquisition, thinking up your points that are focused on the question, using SPEEDL to expand these points into a sophisticated and detailed answer to the question; I will do the first point excellently.

* That is how to hack any AO1 question.

5. Yes, No, Maybe

AO2

For AO2, you use SPEEDL too but you focus on - "Argument"; "range of views and showing understanding" with "critical analysis" (Does 1 + 1 = 2?); and "an evaluation/conclusion" that is supported by the whole or at least half of the essay. You don't need to explain, just evaluate. Most of the time you need to say what you think but try to keep and "I think" to the end. When you want to say what you think during the rest of the essay, use other people's voices or the third person. So "Aquinas might argue…" and "someone could say…" or "It might appear…" and so on (see below). You don't have to be strict with this, you can say what you think, but limit it and then at the end DEFINITELY say what you actually think (as long as your mark scheme and specification wants this).

You should see if you think about it, that to any question that is like "What do you think of this?" there is always, 3 answers, yes/no/maybe. Even if we mean "I like it, I agree, I think it is good," these are really yes's; and vica versa are no's. You can either then answer as three blocks, "yes, Hume's claims about miracles are strong for these reasons blah blah blah;" then "no, Hume's claims are not strong…blah blah blah," followed by "Perhaps, his claims are in between, semi convincing…blah blah blah" ending with a conclusion either way on what you think, finally, about the claim in the question.

Alternatively, and more sophisticatedly, you could answer as a table tennis match, knocking fors, and againsts, back and forth. This is preferred, but it is harder to do. A good trick is to use the textbook, philosophers and scholars, as your voice, so you have a potential of four voices, saying yes and no, back and forth. For example, *"Can anything be good?"*:

"Aquinas, says that good is what is natural, and he looks to natural laws to explain what is good. On the other hand, Ayer's version of emotivism suggests that what is good is only an emotional preference by biological entities, so perhaps nothing can be good. Alternatively, Brandt argues against emotivism and suggest moral statements like "good" are factual. One could argue that there can be such a thing as "good" as there are more theories and people saying there is than there isn't." Ok, it's a bit crude, but I hope you get the idea.

Here is an example model AO2 essay, inspired by an Edexcel, old course question, 12 marks:

"The ontological argument must be a weak argument for God's existence. Discuss."

Many people argue that the Ontological Argument must be a weak argument due to the failure of its premises, which mean that we cannot deduce its conclusion from them and the argument as a whole collapses and fails to prove God's existence.

One of the major criticisms of the Ontological Argument surrounds the view of existence as a predicate. This is pointed out by Kant via his analogy of the 100 silver thaler. Kant purports that if we take two bags of 100 silver coins, one existing de re and one existing in intellectu alone, neither bag has "more" coins. The ontological argument therefore ultimately fails as we can disprove the premise that existence in intellectu and de re is greater than existence in intellectu alone, as existence is not a "great-making quality" and bestows nothing additional upon those who hold it.

Supporters of the Ontological Argument may purport that this problem is solved by Norman Malcolm, who avoids the problems of existence as a predicate via his Possible Worlds argument. Instead of viewing existence as a maximally great quality which God should hold, Malcolm points out that His existence can be viewed as one of three things – impossible, possible or necessary. This is true of all beings, however a maximally great being ought to have the quality of having a necessary existence rather than having a possible or impossible existence.

Detractors such as Guanilo would counter Malcolm by pointing out the logical flaws in the view that we are able to logically deduce God's existence as a necessary being via his definition as being supremely perfect. Guanilo utilises his "perfect island" analogy to this purpose: we can just as easily conceive of a "supreme [noun]", in this case a supremely perfect island, as we can conceive of a supremely perfect God. Obviously, such a perfect island does not actually exist despite the fact that we can imagine it. This is obviously a flaw in the logic of the argument as it shows the logical gap in the intellectu perception of something as perfect and its de re existence, as accepting this logic allows a host of other, absurdist conclusions.

Aquinas's views of religious language can be utilised to further dismantle the ontological argument by pointing out that the view of God's existence as defined by Anselm is fundamentally flawed. This is in its very attempt to define God - an infinite being cannot be defined by finite beings such as humans, and therefore A Priori arguments about God's existence are doomed to fail.

Ultimately, an assessment of the various strengths and weaknesses of the Ontological Argument allows us to determine that although accepting all of the arguments premises does prove God to be a necessary being, the faults in its premises leave us unable to do so. The most devastating criticisms to the Ontological Argument of all is the view that its conclusion merely gives the name God to a maximally great being, without proving anything about His qualities or that He is the Judeo-Christian God. In this sense, the argument proves most useful for justification by existing believers rather than for proving God's existence in its own right. Therefore, the ontological argument must be a weak argument for the existence of God.

Here's a detailed plan for *"Assess the debate between Copleston and Russell as an argument for or against the existence of God."* (Inspired by an Edexcel A2, new course question, 12 marks):

* Good as an argument, Copleston v Russell (S), There has to be a beginning (P), no infinite regress (E), Checkmate quote (E), makes sense, dominoes (D), it is possible God is the beginning (L)
* Bad as an argument, Copleston v Russell (S), There has to be a reason for everything (P), everything has an explanation (E), who made God (E), it's more normal to think there is an explanation (D), God doesn't seem like a good explanation (L)
* Good as an argument Russell v Copleston (S), it is possible that God doesn't have a mother (P), God could be a different category (E), the Big-Bang didn't have a mother (E), ontologically this could suggest God is the cause of the Big Bang (D), this is a good argument for the existence of God (L)
* Bad as an argument Russel v Copleston (S), there is no point discussing it (P), it's pointless to find a reason for the existence of the universe (E), as Popper says, we cannot prove anything (E), we really do have to agree to disagree (D), this mimics the parable of the invisible gardener and so suggests it's not a good argument for God (L)
* Conclude

Now again, this is a crude example, yours needs to be much more like the model essay, but I hope it simplifies and universalises it a little bit more. You don't need to follow it exactly like this. **I cannot stress enough how more important it is to simply understand all this and see how you can apply it yourself, rather than trying to match exactly what I say. All the mark schemes and specifications are different. It's therefore HUGELY IMPORTANT THAT YOU READ YOUR MARK SCHEME AND SPECIFICATION! Then think about it and try to merge your requirements and own style to what I say. I hope you can see all that from the model essays too!**

Here is another plan, inspired by an AQA, AS, new course question, 15 marks:

"In making moral decisions, Natural Law is not effective. Assess this claim."

1. it is effective as it is simple, primary precepts and deontology
2. It is focused on reason, nature or what is natural, and so is simple, universal and effective
3. secondary precepts make it flexible, applicable and effective
4. double effect makes its flexible and effective
5. what else about it makes it effective for making moral decisions
6. it is NOT effective - primary and secondary is confusing
7. NOT effective - reason/nature is not universal
8. NOT effective - double effect is confusing
9. NOT effective - what else about it makes it ineffective?
10. Is it effective or not? Conclusion

Note that as it is 15 marks, (and the one above is 12) these would not need to be large paragraphs (like the model AO2 full essay above); **remember, always temper the amount you write with what the marks are…**

One more model essay, linked to the AO1 above, "A*", inspired by an Edexcel, A2, old course question – 20 minutes

"These three arguments are all equally weak. Comment on this claim."

These arguments could be argued to not be equally weak although there is certainly degrees of weakness between them and some of the arguments are weaker than others.

The claim about order and purpose suggesting the existence of God is weak. There are some strong elements to the idea. For example, as Aquinas shows in his analogy of the archer, that order and purpose or "bodies obeying natural laws" was when they lack awareness, must have been directed to that goal by someone with awareness and understanding. It does seem logical and intuitive since we always see an author of order and purpose (for example a watch). However, as Hume pointed out, just because there is a continual conjunction of a designer when we see order and purpose, it doesn't mean all order and purpose has a creator. Previously, this idea seemed to explain why animals and plants are programmed or driven to stay alive and behave and look the way they do. However, Darwin's theory of evolution, which is now supported by large amounts of evidence, suggests a better understanding or the apparent order and purpose and shows how order and purpose are brought about by millions of years of random events. It now seems more plausible that this natural selection is the author rather than a God. Conversely, the anthropic principle is not explained away by evolution but it suggests a precedent for random events to create order and purpose so perhaps the universe is, as Russel says, a brute fact and we are just lucky that it is this way.

Related to this, is the second claim that the design argument is based on empirical data. As we have seen, observations of the world can lead us to logical conclusions that are in fact, wrong. Focusing on things that seem far too complex, purposed and "designed", like the eye, does seem to be best explained by a designer. If the eye was "created" by random acts, how did it go from not useful (as it would have been before it was fully developed) to the amazingly useful and developed thing it is today? A designer guiding this development is more intuitive and seems to make more sense. This, however, again falls foul to evolution. Just because we can observe something that appears a certain way, doesn't mean it is. As Hume shows, if it is so perfectly designed, why do humans not see all colors of the spectrum or through walls? It is possible the things we observe were created by a juvenile or mischievous God (particularly if we look at the problem of evil). As Hume showed in his analogy of weights, we cannot necessarily infer the Judeo Christian God from what we observe, and that observation is critically limited as a tool of discovery. This idea therefore seems equally weak as the first one.

The third argument, and perhaps the strongest one, is Tennant's aesthetic principle. Tennant used this argument in avoiding criticisms from Darwinism as beauty is shown to have no real value or purpose, but for the pleasure of those who live on the world, and God himself. But of course, not everyone would agree that beauty of the world points to the existence of God. Some argue beauty is not an absolute quality, but is a matter of opinion, so that beauty does not exist in the sense that Plato's form of beauty might be said to exist but is a value- judgment. Another reason for this argument to be considered weak is the question of where this beauty fits in to John Stuart Mills' criticisms on evil and suffering being designed in the world for example, Mills observed how some plants have features which help suffocate other plants in order to gain maximum light and nutrients. Mill saw things like this in the world as unnecessarily cruel, which begs the question where is beauty in these situations?

To conclude, I do not agree that all three ideas are equally weak, but that Tennant's aesthetic principle has some solid ground in its reasoning for beauty, but that the ideas of both design and purpose can easily be discredited by the likes of Hume and Darwin's theory of evolution.

That's it, it's quite simple and AO2, which is almost wholly focused on the evaluation, the argument, the views, and the comment, is normally always preferred by students because it doesn't need as much knowledge. Blaggers also do well on these.

For longer essays you need to expand on the flipping and flopping, back and forth; give more views, disagree with yourself and look at it from other peoples' shoes, expand on the analysis, the criticising, the agreeing, the disagreeing. Always, starting simple and going deeper.

* Therefore: this is how to hack any AO2 question!

6. For an essay that needs AO1 and AO2 (or AO3) combined

The plan given in the chapter above (*"'Natural Law's strengths are bigger than its weaknesses.' Discuss"* (Inspired by an OCR AS, new course question, 30 marks) is an example of AO1 and AO2 combined. It's a big thing in the new courses so it needs a mention.

On the whole, with these essays, you are doing your AO1 in the beginning when you are defining your terms and laying out the lay of the land, the context and direction, of the essay. Where necessary, you will explain something within the essay also. It depends on your plan and how you will attack the question and how your essay flows.

The main thing to remember is, you follow SPEEDL throughout, in the beginning it will be AO1 heavy, then more AO2 (so you will need "Yes, No, Maybe"). If you encounter something that needs explaining, follow the guidance on AO1. After the beginning, a lot of your essay will be AO2, with AO1 being used to give more information to your argument. Make sure you conclude.

To see how much AO1 and how much AO2 to do, you need to look at the mark scheme and specification; read the next chapters, as appropriate, for details.

At its most basic, you are just mixing the last two chapters (SPEEDL and "Yes, No, Maybe") together into one essay.

AO3, when it is synoptic, just means adding in the occasional reference to some piece of information from another topic in the course, so mentioning something from Utilitarianism (e.g. its similar focus on reason) when you are talking about Natural law. It means finding links between your essay and the topic it is about, to other topics of the course. It can also ask you to link what you found out in AS to your A2 essay.

AO3, when it is other intellectual skills, will be covered if you follow the guidance in this book, it's generally not used but I like to be thorough!

Here is a model mixed essay, note the skilful use of AO1 explaining/showing knowledge and/or understanding, *where necessary to add to the essay*:

<u>"A"/"A*", A2, inspired by an OCR, old course question:</u>

"'Butler's claims that people have an innate sense of right and wrong are not convincing.' Discuss. (35)"

There are conflicting claims about whether the conscience is innate or acquired. When the conscience is referred to as innate, it means that it is inborn within you. From a religious perspective an innate conscience is one which is from God, where our sense of right or wrong is possible from understanding God and his wishes. Often we find the conscience has an important role in our decision making, so its source is of importance to many. Joseph Butler claimed that the conscience comes from God, while psychologists such as Freud, Piaget and Fromm argue that the conscience is acquired from our upbringing and society. So how convincing are Butler's claims of an innate conscience in respects to evil that occurs in the name of the conscience, Christian moral dilemmas, and whether it is then a reliable guide.

Joseph Butler claimed that the conscience was a person's God-given guide to right conduct, its demands therefore must be followed. He spoke of the conscience "magisterially exerting itself" spontaneously "without being consulted". This tells us about the innate way that conscience works. Butler's ideas implies that everyone has an innate sense knowledge of what "good" is. We would therefore expect everyone to have a conscience and for it to work more or less in the same way. As we know many people have different ideas of what "good" is and hold different moral principles. What may seem as evil for some; actions such as child marriages, FGM even terrorism can and have been defended in the name of the conscience. If our conscience is from God and infallible it is questionable that everyone does not know for certain what God commands of them, and from the example that we don't all attain the same standard of right and wrong. Perhaps we should not give the conscience as much reliability as Butler does, as is not as clear cut as it seems, making his argument less convincing.

However, Butler would argue that we are all essentially good but our natural instinct is to look after ourselves. At the same time, we also have a desire to help others and it is the conscience's job to weigh up these two opposing interests of self-love and benevolence. This, for Butler is why during moral decisions we may be uncertain of what to do. The "principle of reflection" which is most linked to the conscience, makes us approve or disprove of our actions; as Butler thinks the conscience will tell you to watch out for others as far as possible, evil acts compromise this idea as they are usually self-orientated. Hence, it would not be seen as the conscience that makes mistakes since it is innately good, but rather a person's self-deception where one convinces them self that their wrong and evil actions are right. It seems convincing that benevolence is in the interest of the conscience because many would agree that our natural sense of good actions depends on looking out for others interests, often over our own. F Hutcherson also agreed, saying it was this natural sense of benevolence that was the source of our morality. For example, our reaction to suffering of others is what drives us look out for humanity. In this line of thinking Butlers claim of an innate sense of right and wrong is convincing since he gives us a criteria of what actions are a result of listening to the conscience and tells us why different people hold different moral principles.

Butler was not interested in whether the conscience was based on reason, feeling or both like many other thinkers, just that its existence is obvious, authoritative and automatic when moral decisions have to be made. However, moral disagreements do occur, even within Christian denominations on issues such as abortion. How reliable is an innate conscience and should we give it the final say in moral decision-making as Butler claims? One main suggestion to why people's moral principles vary is the view that they are acquired from parents, teachers and society. Psychologists such as Sigmund Freud claim that the conscience is a construct of the mind as it is acquired and not innate. Freud completed studies on the human mind and linked the need of religion to obsessional neurosis. Our conscience arises as a result of bad experiences early in life, as well as disapproval from parents and authoritative figures. The superego, a set of moral controls given by outside influences such as teachers becomes conflicted with the amoral ID containing basic drives such as food and sex. We internalise the feelings of guilt and shame we get when we go against these rules, and they then become the basis of our morality. For religious people God becomes the authority and issues such as homosexuality and sex before marriage become condemned, making one guilty if they go against the rules opposed by the church, bible and other authoritarian leaders. While Butler said we must follow the authority of the conscience, Freud would argue against allowing the superego to have control over how we act as it would make you overly judgemental, inflexible and irrational. As Freud also did not believe in absolute moral law, no moral code is constantly right or wrong, so principles are subjective to society. Freud's argument makes it acceptable for people to conflict about different issues making Butlers claims less convincing since the conscience does not necessarily have to come from God.

Jean Piaget a developmental psychologist who expanded the work of Freud claimed that by studying human nature one can see how the conscience develops over time due to social interaction and is therefore not something we are born with. Arguments from both Freud and Piaget point to the origin of the conscience from social interaction and external influences. While it's defiantly a valid argument, others have claimed that explaining the origin of the conscience does not remove its religious significance. Meaning that Butlers claims of an innate sense of right and wrong is still convincing despite attempts to show that it involves interacting with society.

Butler rejected the conscience being something acquired, arguing that if conscience were something learnt then where would its authority come from? People's consciences would develop differently according to where they live and how they were brought up. Looking at the evidence it seems this may be the case. Besides, it could be argued that Butler's theory is too simplistic because it assumes the initial existence of God. Many atheists, agnostics and humanists claim that the conscience is important to them, such claims do not rely of God who is said to regulate the moral order of the universe. This would mean the conscience is a universal part of moral living and is not a God given faculty or special equipment needed to make moral decisions.

Thomas Aquinas's ideas on the conscience advances on Butlers approach since he mentions the importance of reason to work out what actions the conscience is pointing us towards. Rather than the conscience being a voice or something directly from God he believed the conscience was right reason seeking understanding. This right reason also known as synderesis is our God-given innate moral principles that need to be applied to each situation and judgement (conscientia) as best as possible. This requires training as Aquinas accepted that the conscience can err and mistakes when we don't use our reasoning correctly. But ultimately it comes down to the person to educate the conscience to reason correctly and find out what God sees is good. This shows that Butlers claims of an innate conscience is less convincing since it needs to be modified to allow for mistakes and provide a sense of criteria or tools to make decisions.

In conclusion Butler's claims on an innate conscience seem questionable. An infallible authoritarian conscience implies that everyone knows what God commands of them, this does not seem as clear cut as he makes out. A benevolent conscience seems satisfying but, what is seen as the most loving thing is often dependent on society and upbringing. So perhaps the psychologists are right to claim the conscience is not in fact innate but based on external influences. This argument can be seen in everyday behaviour and also accepts that morality is a part of human nature rather than religion. For certain it seems too simplistic to agree with Butler that the conscience is always right and cannot be mistaken. Thomas Aquinas' approach seems to be a medium between the two opposing claims. An innate conscience dependent on reason does not necessarily need to involve God, this allows everyone to be accountable for their actions. His claims also stress the importance of training the conscience and provide the tools to make right decisions. Although they don't lead to a definite answer they led to a correct moral path.

Ok, you've got at least a model example of each now. You should be able to use all these to figure out what *your* essay needs.

For the next few chapters, you only need to read the one about *your* exam board…

7. AQA

Ok, so we know; what we need to know and how to know it, we know the context and how the game works, and we know what to do with our knowledge. What we need to look at now is how all this will be marked, to temper and add to what we have learnt about how to write essays. When I said earlier on, how this is how it all applies; it's because your mark scheme and the marks given is the key to work out how it all applies to *your* essay.

The key thing is that when we read our essays, we need to get the impression or feeling (it's an art, not a science, remember) that it is in the top level of the mark scheme.

I wanted to put in this section a selection of the top levels of the most common, generic mark schemes, as most people will probably be assessed using these and we are aiming for the top. Unfortunately AQA wouldn't give me permission because they "think that your emphasis is too much on improving grades or how to achieve certain grades. AQA grants permission for books covering the whole spectrum of teaching and gaining of skills, rather than examination alone." Doesn't make any sense right? Because they (probably) know that I have produced a hack that ruins their system! They don't want everyone to get an A*, or to know exactly how to improve grades; their exam would be useless if everyone did. Unfortunately, until the educational establishment removes the life importance of these exams, they can't have what they want (and what I want to), that the exam isn't the focus (remember our chapter on Teachers and

Examiners above!). We would all like students to just study and love the subject and gain the skills that are trying to be taught. But the exam is too important for your life to not make it more important than all of that. So, instead, I've given links to some of the key mark schemes.

It's really important that you have a look at what is at the end of these links, but just focus on the top levels. This is one of the most important parts of this book!

However and additionally, every unit could be different, for example in the mark weighting or marks allowed, so **be sure to actually look for your course using the links provided to confirm which mark scheme is being used. Bigger marks will ask for a little bit more in the mark scheme.** Once you know this, then you can still incorporate what I say about the rest of the mark schemes. You will notice these bigger questions bump it up with AO3 objectives for example; it is quite simple once you have a look and understand them. It is one of the key things to get success that you look at, understand and follow the mark scheme; it is what the examiner is looking at when they are marking your work. It is almost like cheating that is allowed; you'd be silly not to have a look! In my day, they just taught us and then gave us an exam, we knew nothing. You, including university students or whatever, have access to so much information that can help you, how to get a top grade, it's nuts that more people don't use this information! It's more nuts that AQA won't let me reprint them here, since you can access it all yourself anyway!

Do you want to help me reform education? Do you want to stick one to the "Man"? Follow this book, tell you friends, get everyone to read this hack; do it right, break the system and we will do it; it's the only way!

AQA's Mark scheme, AS, new course, Religious Studies

The Link –

http://www.aqa.org.uk/subjects/religious-studies/as-and-a-level/religious-studies-7061/assessment-resources

AQA's Mark scheme, A2, new course, Religious Studies

The Link –

http://www.aqa.org.uk/subjects/religious-studies/as-and-a-level/religious-studies-7062/assessment-resources

AQA's Mark scheme, AS & A2, old course, Religious Studies

The Link –

http://www.aqa.org.uk/subjects/religious-studies/as-and-a-level/religious-studies-2060/past-papers-and-mark-schemes

Remember, I have chosen the most common, generic mark scheme. With this last course for example, there are some other mark schemes for some of the other units. They are assessing higher marks, so there is a little bit more in the assessment objectives/criteria. **Be sure to actually look for your course using these links to confirm which mark scheme is being used.**

AQA's Mark scheme, AS, new course, Philosophy

The Link –

http://www.aqa.org.uk/subjects/philosophy/as-and-a-level/philosophy-7171/assessment-resources

AQA's Mark scheme, A2, new course, Philosophy

The Link - http://www.aqa.org.uk/subjects/philosophy/as-and-a-level/philosophy-7172/assessment-resources

AQA's Mark scheme, AS & A2, old(ish) course, Philosophy -

The Link –

http://www.aqa.org.uk/subjects/philosophy/as-and-a-level/philosophy-2175/past-papers-and-mark-schemes

What's the first thing you see? It should be that even though they look completely different, they are actually asking for roughly the same thing. They have to, by law and logic, remember! The main difference is between AO1 and AO2, not between the different marks scheme. Therefore, if you follow ALL the advice of this book, it will work for any essay exam.

The other main difference is that AS and A2 are different because they are asking for a little more. This often means bigger, richer paragraphs. Where a mark scheme is asking for more, say it has a level 4 and another has a level 5, it's again asking for more information, more knowledge and understanding or more comment and analysis, read the mark scheme for precisely what, but it can be dealt with by bigger and richer paragraphs. You're just expanding SPEEDL or "Yes, No, Maybe".

For example, all the AO1s above, they want a thorough, focused, detailed, religious or philosophical, complete, answer to the question. That's SPEEDL. AO2 will be satisfied by "Yes, No, Maybe".

You do have to incorporate the slight differences. E.g. when AO1 and AO2 are mixed (see the chapter above) or for example in the Philosophy for AQA, there is a focus on philosophical language, logic and philosophical communication.

You absolutely must look at the exact mark scheme for your exam using the links. I'm sorry to keep repeating it, but it is that important!

But, if I keep the top level in mind when I am writing my essays, if I read it when I've written it and can see whether it is hitting these criteria, I can KNOW that I will get a top grade. You can now work out how all the things I have said in this book need to look in practice.

8. OCR

Ok, so we know; what we need to know and how to know it, we know the context and how the game works, and we know what to do with our knowledge. What we need to look at now is how all this will be marked, to temper and add to what we have learnt about how to write essays. When I said earlier on, how this is how it all applies; it's because your mark scheme and the marks given is the key to work out how it all applies to *your* essay.

The key thing is that when we read our essays, we need to get the impression or feeling (it's an art, not a science, remember) that it is in the top level of the mark scheme.

I wanted to put in this section a selection of the top levels of the most common, generic mark schemes, as most people will probably be assessed using these and we are aiming for the top. Unfortunately AQA wouldn't give me permission because they "think that your emphasis is too much on improving grades or how to achieve certain grades. AQA grants permission for books covering the whole spectrum of teaching and gaining of skills, rather than examination alone." Once they said no I had to come up with a work around; OCR didn't even reply! Doesn't make any sense right? Because they (probably) know that I have produced a hack that ruins their system! They don't want everyone to get an A*, or to know exactly how to improve grades; their exam would be useless if everyone did. Unfortunately, until the educational establishment removes the life importance of these exams, they can't have what they want (and what I want to), that the exam isn't the focus (remember our chapter on Teachers and Examiners above!). We would all like students to just study and love the subject and gain the skills that are trying to be taught. But the exam is too important for your life to not make it more important than all of that. So, instead, I've given links to some of the key mark schemes.

It's really important that you have a look at what is at the end of these links, but just focus on the top levels. This is one of the most important parts of this book!

However and additionally, every unit could be different, for example in the mark weighting or marks allowed, so **be sure to actually look for your course using the links provided to confirm which mark scheme is being used. Bigger marks will ask for a little bit more in the mark scheme.** Once you know this, then you can still incorporate what I say about the rest of the mark schemes. You will notice these bigger questions bump it up with AO3 objectives for example; it is quite simple once you have a look and understand them. It is one of the key things to get success that you look at, understand and follow the mark scheme; it is what the examiner is looking at when they are marking your work. It is almost like cheating that is allowed; you'd be silly not to have a look! In my day, they just taught us and then gave us an exam, we knew nothing. You, including university students or whatever, have access to so much information that can help you, how to get a top grade, it's nuts that more people don't use this information! It's more nuts that AQA won't let me reprint them here, since you can access it all yourself anyway!

Do you want to help me reform education? Do you want to stick one to the "Man"? Follow this book, tell you friends, get everyone to read this hack; do it right, break the system and we will do it; it's the only way!

OCR's Mark scheme, AS, new course, Religious Studies

The Link –

http://www.ocr.org.uk/qualifications/as-a-level-gce-religious-studies-h173-h573-from-2016/

OCR's Mark scheme, A2, new course, Religious Studies

The Link –

http://www.ocr.org.uk/qualifications/as-a-level-gce-religious-studies-h173-h573-from-2016/

Remember, I have chosen the most common, generic mark scheme. With some courses, there are some other mark schemes for some of the other units. They are assessing higher marks, so there is a little bit more in the assessment objectives/criteria. **Be sure to actually look for your course using these links to confirm which mark scheme is being used.**

OCR's Mark scheme, AS, old course, Religious Studies

The Link –

http://www.ocr.org.uk/qualifications/as-a-level-gce-religious-studies-h172-h572/

OCR's Mark scheme, A2, old course, Religious Studies

The Link –

http://www.ocr.org.uk/qualifications/as-a-level-gce-religious-studies-h172-h572/

What's the first thing you see? It should be that even though they look completely different, they are actually asking for roughly the same thing. They have to, by law and logic, remember! The main difference is between AO1 and AO2, not between the different marks scheme. Therefore, if you follow ALL the advice of this book, it will work for any essay exam.

The other main difference is that AS and A2 are different because they are asking for a little more. This often means bigger, richer paragraphs. Where a mark scheme is asking for more, say it has a level 4 and another has a level 5, it's again asking for more information, more knowledge and understanding or more comment and analysis, read the mark scheme for precisely what, but it can be dealt with by bigger and richer paragraphs. You're just expanding SPEEDL or "Yes, No, Maybe".

For example, all the AO1s above, they want a thorough, focused, detailed, religious or philosophical, complete, answer to the question. That's SPEEDL. AO2 will be satisfied by "Yes, No, Maybe".

You do have to incorporate the slight differences. E.g. when AO1 and AO2 are mixed (see the chapter above) or for example in the Philosophy for AQA, there is a focus on philosophical language, logic and philosophical communication.

You absolutely must look at the exact mark scheme for your exam using the links. I'm sorry to keep repeating it, but it is that important!

But, if I keep the top level in mind when I am writing my essays, if I read it when I've written it and can see whether it is hitting these criteria, I can KNOW that I will get a top grade. You can now work out how all the things I have said in this book need to look in practice.

9. EDEXCEL

Ok, so we know; what we need to know and how to know it, we know the context and how the game works, and we know what to do with our knowledge. What we need to look at now is how all this will be marked, to temper and add to what we have learnt about how to write essays. When I said earlier on, how this is how it all applies; it's because your mark scheme and the marks given is the key to work out how it all applies to *your* essay.

The key thing is that when we read our essays, we need to get the impression or feeling (it's an art, not a science, remember) that it is in the top level of the mark scheme.

I wanted to put in this section a selection of the top levels of the most common, generic mark schemes, as most people will probably be assessed using these and we are aiming for the top. Unfortunately AQA wouldn't give me permission because they "think that your emphasis is too much on improving grades or how to achieve certain grades. AQA grants permission for books covering the whole spectrum of teaching and gaining of skills, rather than examination alone." Once they said no I had to come up with a work around; Edexcel replied at first but then didn't reply giving or forbidding me permission. Doesn't make any sense right? Because they (probably) know that I have produced a hack that ruins their system! They don't want everyone to get an A*, or to know exactly how to improve grades; their exam would be useless if everyone did. Unfortunately, until the educational establishment removes the life importance of these exams, they can't have what they want (and what I want to), that the exam isn't the focus (remember our chapter on Teachers and Examiners above!). We would all like students to just study and love the subject and gain the skills that are trying to be taught. But the exam is too important for your life to not make it more important than all of that. So, instead, I've given links to some of the key mark schemes.

It's really important that you have a look at what is at the end of these links, but just focus on the top levels. This is one of the most important parts of this book!

However and additionally, every unit could be different, for example in the mark weighting or marks allowed, so **be sure to actually look for your course using the links provided to confirm which mark scheme is being used. Bigger marks will ask for a little bit more in the mark scheme.** Once you know this, then you can still incorporate what I say about the rest of the mark schemes. You will notice these bigger questions bump it up with AO3 objectives for example; it is quite simple once you have a look and understand them. It is one of the key things to get success that you look at, understand and follow the mark scheme; it is what the examiner is looking at when they are marking your work. It is almost like cheating that is allowed; you'd be silly not to have a look! In my day, they just taught us and then gave us an exam, we knew nothing. You, including university students or whatever, have access to so much information that can help you, how to get a top grade, it's nuts that more people don't use this information! It's more nuts that AQA won't let me reprint them here, since you can access it all yourself anyway!

Do you want to help me reform education? Do you want to stick one to the "Man"? Follow this book, tell you friends, get everyone to read this hack; do it right, break the system and we will do it; it's the only way!

Edexcel's Mark scheme, AS, new course, Religious Studies

The Link –

https://qualifications.pearson.com/en/qualifications/edexcel-a-levels/religious-studies-2016.coursematerials.html

Edexcel's Mark scheme, A2, new course, Religious Studies

The Link –

https://qualifications.pearson.com/en/qualifications/edexcel-a-levels/religious-studies-2016.coursematerials.html

Edexcel's Mark scheme, AS, old course, Religious Studies

The Link –

https://qualifications.pearson.com/en/qualifications/edexcel-a-levels/religious-studies-2008.coursematerials.html

Remember, I have chosen the most common, generic mark scheme. With some courses, there are some other mark schemes for some of the other units. They are assessing higher marks, so there is a little bit more in the assessment objectives/criteria. **Be sure to actually look for your course using these links to confirm which mark scheme is being used.**

Edexcel's Mark scheme, A2, old course, Religious Studies

The Link –

https://qualifications.pearson.com/en/qualifications/edexcel-a-levels/religious-studies-2008.coursematerials.html

What's the first thing you see? It should be that even though they look completely different, they are actually asking for roughly the same thing. They have to, by law and logic, remember! The main difference is between AO1 and AO2, not between the different marks scheme. Therefore, if you follow ALL the advice of this book, it will work for any essay exam.

The other main difference is that AS and A2 are different because they are asking for a little more. This often means bigger, richer paragraphs. Where a mark scheme is asking for more, say it has a level 4 and another has a level 5, it's again asking for more information, more knowledge and understanding or more comment and analysis, read the mark scheme for precisely what, but it can be dealt with by bigger and richer paragraphs. You're just expanding SPEEDL or "Yes, No, Maybe".

For example, all the AO1s above, they want a thorough, focused, detailed, religious or philosophical, complete, answer to the question. That's SPEEDL. AO2 will be satisfied by "Yes, No, Maybe".

You do have to incorporate the slight differences. E.g. when AO1 and AO2 are mixed (see the chapter above) or for example in the Philosophy for AQA, there is a focus on philosophical language, logic and philosophical communication.

You absolutely must look at the exact mark scheme for your exam using the links. I'm sorry to keep repeating it, but it is that important!

But, if I keep the top level in mind when I am writing my essays, if I read it when I've written it and can see whether it is hitting these criteria, I can KNOW that I will get a top grade. You can now work out how all the things I have said in this book need to look in practice.

10. Revision

Revision can be hacked too. We are limited by our working memory, it can hold between 3 and 7 bits of information at once; on the whole. We are also limited by our long term memory, in that if you don't use it, you lose it. But both can be trained and worked with.

Short term memory can be trained and extended by practicing things that work it and extend it, like puzzles, crosswords, essays and other brain training things.

Long term memory can be trained and solidified through repetition and using. You remember how to brush your teeth because you do it (hopefully) every day. So, practicing something can ensure it is in your memory, but using it (see the chapter "Practice") is key: *knowing the point of knowing it,* remember our Ikea instruction booklet!

Now, again, we can take shortcuts here. We can also use neurology and related information to help us.

Mind maps can help us further with short term memory, as can practice essays. But a few facts can help us further with the long term: a child's concentration ranges from 15-45 minutes, increasing as you increase in age. An adult's brain is more like 30 minutes to an hour, depending on their training. This means revision sessions of more than 30 minutes to 45 minutes are pointless. You won't remember it, on the whole.

Also, a lot of research says that if you revise or study for 30 mins, then do something completely unrelated, like make a cup of tea, go for a short walk, or whatever, for about 5 minutes and then go and revise for another 30 minutes, and do this on and on for about 6-8 hours; it's the best way to remember stuff and revise. It's working with your brain and will naturally help you focus and get the most out of your revision.

Additionally, if I receive information in my head once, then the next day I receive it again and a week later again and a month later again and then, 3 months later, the finally, just before I need it; again: this is the best way to remember stuff. It's how homework is supposed to work.

Therefore, if I listen in class, engage, do my homeworks, have a weekly slot for doing my knowledge acquisition, use mind maps, and then revise, early on and then again nearer the exam and I do it in 30 minute chunks, also practicing essays and focusing on the question; I will allow my brain the best chance at remembering information and it will be more natural and stress free than any other revision technique. It will also satisfy the need to train my long term memory and will tick the box for repetition as well as using it.

So using your mind maps and practice essays, early on if possible, combined with your school work, in 30 minute chunks, taking a five minute, unrelated break, using a revision guide (they are worth having) and testing yourself or with a friend (another thing that has been proven to work better than any other revision technique): that is how to hack revision.

A good diet, drinking water, exercising, meditating, having play time and a good rest should all be a part of your daily life; if you want to maximise your potential. While you are revising taking naps actually helps the brain consolidate, process and remember stuff so they are recommended too! Kids need more sleep than adults anyway. If you think about it, it's an easy win, you will be healthy, fit and at your optimum and do well in your exams!

The night before the exam just chill if possible (meditation is great!), have some fun, exercise a little, have a good rest and sleep, and then have another quick look at stuff in the morning. Drink some water to keep you hydrated but not too much you need to pee! (Drinking regular small amounts of water has been shown to improve intelligence, memory and concentration.) Eat well if possible, your brain needs fuel, and hunger can disturb you but also an empty stomach *can* lead to higher focus so if you can't eat, don't worry too much!

11. Practice

I hated hearing "practice makes perfect" because I always found it really hard to practice. There doesn't seem to be a point and it's "long"!

Unfortunately there *is* a point, and it *is* a true statement. If you make it a part of your regular study, as I've suggested above, it doesn't have to be "long". **You simply *have to* practice essays** so you can keep improving and see, in reality, the guidance in this book and how you are doing as measured to it. Only when you have a go, can you see where you are, and only by keep having goes and improving every time, can you perfect it. You are doing an essay exam and so it's an easy win to practice those essays; look at the Chapter on "Questions" below to help.

Again, these should be timed, but in the beginning be more generous with your time, getting to the exam standard from January before the exam.

I am sure your teacher would love to mark extra essays, they kind of have to in my opinion, and it's in their interests and yours to do so. You can email me at andrew@commonsensible.org too and I can do it, though I charge (GBP) £10 an essay (or foreign currency equivalent).

So yeah, practice does make perfect, damn it!

12. Exam skills/The actual exam

In the actual exam you should be calm (seriously, try meditation, it really helps) but also use the adrenaline to your advantage, it will help you think and write quicker. Read the question and make sure you answer the same question and not one you think you saw because you've gone "panic or overconfidence-blind". Focus on the actual question and be strict with your time allowed per essay.

Because you should have done so many practice essays, you will know how much you are writing and how long you are writing for. You will not finish early or late and you will not waste a second.

Read the chapter on "Questions" below.

You must make sure your equipment is sorted and that nothing slows you down.

Do not plan or make a very quick one.

If you cannot finish bullet point what you were going to say, but also conclude to, linked to the question. It can still be marked to some extent (it's better than nothing!) for most boards.

However, be confident, you've got this!

You've got good knowledge from the knowledge acquisition and revision. You know what to do with it in an essay. You know how you are being marked and what they are looking for. You are ready!

13. Questions (and When AO1 looks like AO2)

Ok, sometimes examiners are total douche bags and they ask an AO1 question that looks like you are supposed to evaluate it. The example essay in the chapter on SPEEDL is an example (as is the model essay in the same chapter):

"The ontological argument must be a strong argument for God's existence. Examine this claim."

Looks like you're supposed to assess it, like an AO2 doesn't it. It led many students down the wrong path the year it was used in an exam.

So the first thing is READ THE FLIPPING QUESTION GUYS! But the second thing is, make sure you are explaining *only* in AO1 and evaluating *only* in AO2. Pay attention to whether it is AO1 or AO2, it will normally say or you will know from practice!

Therefore, for this example you need to state why someone, but not you, might say it is a strong argument, explain all about it without getting into discussion. The model essay on this question above handles it wonderfully. Speak factually and focus on the question wording. Just avoid saying "what you think" in AO1 questions is a good approach, that "saying what you think" is purely reserved for AO2 questions.

More importantly, Questions!

You know, on reflection, if the exam is about asking you about the controversy within the bodies of knowledge you are studying, if it is about the significant parts, the "tell me what is a pen" parts; there is a limit to how many questions can be asked.

All they can really do is play with the words or focus on different things.

So on religious language, I can only really be asked about the sense, or nonsense of it, the verifiability or non-verifiability of it, on the symbols, analogy, language games of it and so on. There is a limit.

It's also why some years some questions look very different to another, when really they are the same question worded in a different way. It can be reversed or demand you talk about stuff that doesn't seem immediately obvious from the question.

But information wise, as long as I can pin the information to the question, it will be valid and relevant.

So, I can be on top of the questions completely if I just spent some time thinking of some of my own.

You can work these out for yourself by looking at the past questions, knowing the course well and giving it some thought. The past papers are available for anyone to see using the links for the mark schemes above.

You should put this on your mindmaps and you should practice these as essays.

It is a critical practice that will really give you the edge for that A*. An edge, because no-one, not even I, can guarantee you an A*, not really. All we can do is limit the things that stand in the way, do our best and hope for the best!

14. Lastminute.com

Just so you know, almost all teachers hate people like you . However, being one of the Lastminute.com club too, I've got some good help for you!

If it is before the end of Spring term holiday and you still haven't revised, it is still not too late.

Beyond this point, you are pushing it, but you do still have a chance. In fact, some people could probably revise and remember everything in two or three weeks. The teacher inside me hates to admit it, but it is possible.

HOWEVER, this is so rare and so out of the reach of most students that it is to most people impossible.

Since we are about removing all the obstacles that stand in our way, *not being a lastminute.commer.* is the best approach.

But, being a realist as I am, this is what you should do if you are really behind:

Still do the mind maps and revise, failing that just revise, read SPEEDL and "Yes, No, Maybe" and as much of this book as you can. Read the mark scheme, specification and look at possible questions/past papers. Try to follow this book's guidance but: be vague (if it's vague it has less chance of being wrong), use paraphrasing and focus on what you or someone *could* say, if you can't say enough. If it is relevant to the question it is credit worthy even if it is information I wouldn't expect to see. You will find AO2 easier than AO1 (as it is discussion based and we can all have a discussion on a page!) but often there are more marks for AO1 so you want to do your best with both, even if you don't know enough.

How to blag it properly? With enough relevant info, focused on the question, this is how you blag it. Therefore, it doesn't *necessarily* matter what the info is, as long as it is relevant. That does often mean it has to be philosophical or religious, but it does allow for other info too.

Finally, it is always worth answering a question instead of leaving it blank.

15. If it all goes wrong

The truth is, and to contradict myself, it really doesn't matter. So what, if you don't get into the university you wanted, or got the grade you thought you would or whatever: in 10 years neither you nor anyone else will remember or care about these exams or what you got, they won't even care what university you went to or if you did at all. Life is not just about academic attainment, it is not all about work or what job you do. It is about being happy.

Going to university, doing well, being excellent and so on, all help you to be happy, they are still worth pursuing. But, mistakes happen, things go wrong and life isn't perfect. So if all that stuff, if it makes you unhappy, just forget about it and move on. There's lots of amazing things out there in the world, amazing things to see and do and try; you will find your way whatever happens, as long as you focus on being happy, positive and getting on with it.

You could try and get a remark, it sometimes makes sense.

But there's a lot to be said for doing your best and then moving on to something else if it all goes wrong. Life is short, it might be the only one you've got, so focus on being happy, not on exams and what the system wants of you.

16. It doesn't matter what the knowledge is

Here's an esoteric chapter for you. If you can understand that this system can be applied to any question, because it is built on universals (though it might need tweaking), then you can get this.

AO1 -

Tell me about 1,2,3,4,5.

Answer =

1,2,3,4,5 is…

1 blah, blah, blah

2 blah, blah, blah

3 blah, blah, blah

4 blah, blah, blah

5 blah, blah, blah

This is what is 1,2,3,4,5

AO2 -

"1 and 3 are crap, discuss."

Yes 1 and 3 are crap, blah, blah, blah

No 1 and 3 are not crap, blah, blah, blah

Actually it's 2 and 4 that are crap, blah, blah, blah

Then again, it might be 5, blah, blah, blah

Then again maybe 1 and 3 are crap, blah, blah, blah

On balance I think they are quite crap but 5 is worse.

Seriously, understand this and you can apply this system to any subject that needs a textual response!

In a formalised way, it is:

The answer or the top grade (x) = Question (q) / knowledge (z) + this system (y)!

To show this in an actual essay, here is a politics AO1 one, doing all the things I argue for in this book. This one is not quite there yet, but it is really close. This particular student was doing "D" grade essays and then spending a week with my system, he produced this! My feedback in capitals shows the minor things it needs to improve further.

"Explain the "war on terror" and how it differs from more traditional warfare?" 15 marks

The war on terror is the ongoing campaign by the United States and some of its allies to counter international terrorism. The war on terror was first declared by the US president George bush on the September 20th 2001. George Bush claimed that the war was "freedom vs fear" and that it was a global war against terrorism. This global war AGAINST ANTI-WESTERN TERRORISTS can be seen by how the US lead the war in both Afghanistan and in Iraq leading to the attack on terror and the claimed "liberation" of both countries. More recently the war has no longer been war amongst countries but has become a united war against terrorism. The war on terror has significantly changed after the death of Osama Bin-laden, as the heat of the war front shifted from al-Qaeda in north eastern Asia to ISIS in the middle east specifically Syria. The level of change from this type of war and the war that was faced traditionally by countries has now changed as the enemy is now more difficult to differentiate between the enemy and civilians, whereas in traditional warfare it was always clear who the enemy was making the type of warfare more direct and efficient. Currently the US and its allies such as the UK are using drones to strike down terrorists and amongst those attacks more civilians have perished. This illustrates that the war on terror is different from traditional wars, due the enemy being unknown, and the enemy being on a global scale rather than having a defined territory. AND CIVILIANS; ALWAYS SUM UP THE WHOLE PARAGRAPH IN THE LINK SENTENCE TO BE THOROUGH AND CLEAR. YOU MISSED AN OPPORTUNITY FOR TECHNOLOGY.

Another way in which the war on terror is separate from traditional wars, IS BECAUSE the category of 'new wars' has been applied to conflicts particularly since the mid 1980s by Kaldor. These wars are not fought between nation states but rather wars fought against ideologies and beliefs leading to Huntington's thesis on the clash of civilisations. These wars no longer have to be international but may also be civil wars WHICH HAVE BEEN COMMON IN THE 20TH CENTURY. The war on terror is SIMILAR TO THIS AND IS an asymmetric war meaning that it is a war which is fought where onesie ONE SIDE has a distinct advantage over the other in terms of military might, which would essentially lead to guerrilla tactics from the side which has a disadvantage. An example of asymmetric warfare can be seen in the 9/11 terror attacks the idea of crashing a plane in the world trade centre is an unusual tactic, showing that the war on terror is now different from traditional wars. Another example of guerrilla warfare can be seen by the Paris suicide bombings where three terrorists, blew themselves up in order to strike France in a backlash of them using drones to attack terror groups in the middle east. This once again shows that the way in which the war on terror differs from traditional wars is that there is more of a use of guerrilla warfare and that it is a war against ideology rather than war against a nation AND IT HAS OTHER FEATURES, LIKE CROSSING BORDERS, THAT MAKES IT DIFFERENT TO TRADITIONAL WARS…LINKS TO NEXT PARAGRAPH

Another way in which the war on terror has now differs DIFFERED from traditional warfare is through the fact that THE war on terror is now fought against non-state actors. This war on terror is held against radical Islamism and is seen as a war of fearmongering, due to the fear that terror groups are able to install in the enemy population. The civilians of states such as America after the events of September 11th 2001, were in a state of anxiety and fear of when the next attack was going to happen. This has changed from traditional warfare in which there was a distinct separation between armies which fought against each other. This suggests that the level of change between the "war on terror" and traditional wars is quite significant. THIS LAST PARAGRAPH NEEDS A BIT OF EXANDING – SEE BELOW. ALSO, READABILITY, IT IS A BIT ROBOTIC, IT NEEDS TO FLOW MORE.

Ok, I'll save you an AO2 example, I want to keep this book short, but just follow the rest of the guidance, tweak it to your course if necessary, and then watch your grades improve! So, now it's up to you to work out how this book can work for you in whatever essay subject you are doing! **It's up to you to do the study, follow this guidance, practice and then get ready for a top grade! Good luck!**

17. Recommended websites and reading

Some good websites to use –

Knowledge help:

http://plato.stanford.edu/

http://www.iep.utm.edu/

Wikipedia is normally fine too

www.rsrevision.com

www.tes.com

www.Youtube.com

www.slideshare.net

www.alevelphilosophy.co.uk

www.prezi.com

The exam boards websites also have information and some resources

Also searching Google using the advanced feature, you can tell it to only return PowerPoints (ppt) for example

Some schools have dedicated websites which you can access through Google too

Google scholar is a good resource too

Other help:

https://revisionworld.com/ (has a forum too)

http://www.thestudentroom.co.uk/ (has a forum too)

Some good books…just follow these links and have a good search –

Philosophy: (General) http://amzn.to/2f3P1Vk (A-level) http://amzn.to/2f3ObYP

Ethics: (Gen) http://amzn.to/2f3RKOD (A-level) http://amzn.to/2f3JXAt

Religious studies: (Gen) http://amzn.to/2f3QRWw (A-level) http://amzn.to/2f3Qivy

18. About the Author

Andrew Yiallouros is an educationalist, creative and chef and has been working in education since 2007. He mixes his many interests and experiences with his lessons and schemes of work and these have been called outstanding by his peers and Ofsted. He is an innovator and activist and is dedicated to bringing an education to all. See "www.commonsensensible.org"" From www.bittersuite.org.uk

"Hi Andrew, I just wanted to say thank-you for having brought some much-needed inspiration to COLA-I this year…Best wishes, C"

"Thanks for your hard work and enthusiasm with the food technology lessons." C

"I got 80% in my politics, that is because you helped me a lot, thanks a lot!" A

"Ofsted loved the Jesus in Art lessons!" T

"Please don't leave you're everyone's favourite teacher, you make learning fun"… "you taught me life has a meaning..."

"I basically wanted just to thank you sir for being such a good teacher, we all miss your lessons here."

"Rating: 5/5, Within a few months of tutoring with Andrew, I was able to improve my D grades to A grade work in philosophy and politics. Andrew has great knowledge in these subjects and is able to simplify hard topics. As an examiner, he was able to solve my difficulty in understanding the vague mark schemes and finding model answers. Andrew showed me exactly what an A* essay looks like and how I can achieve it by correcting my essays and turning them into model answers himself. This made me realise how achieving A/A* grades is much easier than I thought!

This was also my first experience of online tutoring, I was very sceptical at first but quickly realised how time saving and useful it can be. I am still able to handwrite essays and receive feedback from Andrew by email before even starting the hourly skype sessions. This way I feel supported throughout the whole week."

"Hi, I got all A*s! Thank you so much for your tuition and I would recommend you to anyone..."

"I got my results yesterday and everything went better than expected, I got 100 UMS for both Philosophy and Ethics!" T

"Andrew Yiallouros tutored my son in his first year at Sussex University in International Relations. His Attitude was professional, his time-keeping was good, his grasp of the subject strong and he was a warm and effective tutor, friendly as well as efficient. I would recommend him as a personal tutor or teacher." Philippa Gregory (Author)

The End!